I Escaped the Grip of the Grim Reaper

Into a New and Beautiful Life

robert alan lee

Copyright © 2013 robert alan lee
All rights reserved.

ISBN: 1-4752-6126-8
ISBN-13: 9781475261264

PREFACE

This true and compelling story is told by the author Robert Lee, "In his own words" about a common ordinary man having a run of bad luck by a fire that destroys his business then one day he dies from eating too much cake and ice cream at his home in North Carolina and it all turns into the best thing that could ever possibly happen!

I Escaped the Grip of the Grim Reaper Into a New and Beautiful Life.

Chapter 1: The Beginning!

Hello, my name is Robert Lee and I'd like to share my story with you!

I guess I will start from the beginning! I was born in a small town seven or so miles east of Pittsburgh, Pennsylvania in one of those so called historic towns named after a somewhat famous general by the name of **Edward Braddock, a British general who died from the wounds of battle during the French and Indian war in 1775.**

Once the home of famous industrialists like the Carnegie's who hold claim of building the first Carnegie library in Braddock and Andrew W. Mellon, a philanthropist, art collector, the secretary of the treasury under three different presidents, and also abanker. This one mile long and half of a mile wide track of land was once one of the richest towns per capita of wealth anywhere in the United States in the 1950's! When people would say that they were going 'Downtown,' they didn't mean Pittsburgh, they meant Braddock!

During the Christmas holidays of the 1960's when I was just a kid, I would see the most fantastic decorations and lights strewn all across the telephone poles down the entire length of Braddock Avenue. There were huge red bells, big Noel signs and large green wreaths, and at the end of Braddock Avenue you could admire a huge Santa figure riding his sled with his seven reindeer on the lawn of the Braddock U.S. Steel Headquarters right across the street of the Edgar Thompson steel mill.

When I was just a couple years of age the Talbot Towers were built at the east end of Braddock down by the Monongahela River on Washington street, a low income housing plan of five tall buildings were erected. These buildings named A Building, B Building and so forth, brought to Braddock many un-desirable people. Crime rose to a very high pitch. Then new technology of manufacturing steel caused the layoff of more than one half of its employees.

Once a town with a population of well over eighteen thousand people, today Braddock is a wasteland; Most of the houses and buildings are either torn down or abandoned, even the huge Braddock Hospital where I was born was also torn down in 2010. This hospital was for the most part the main tax revenue for the town. Today there are less than three thousand people residing there.

There was a low budget Levi's Jean commercial filmed in 2009, showing this waste land and what the mayor John Fetterman had in mind to rebuild and re-energize Braddock. The commercial was televised for maybe a year, and then in 2012, there was a movie filmed there,

"Out of the Furnace," starring Christian Bale, and Woody Harrelson from the hit series, 'Cheers' and the movie, 'White men can't jump'; in which an old friend of mine by the name of Jimmy Chusko also has a stand-in part as a prison guard.

I grew up, as the famous boxer and spokes-man for his George Forman grill would say, "po" meaning that his Mama 'as he put it' was so poor, she couldn't afford the letter 'r' in the word poor!

With an absentee and alcoholic father, my mother and us four kids all lived at one time in a third floor apartment above a bar and a 'greasy spoon,' restaurant called, "Tom's."

There was a grocery store right across the parking lot from our building and if I can recall, it was an old 'Giant Eagle' grocery store. Today it's a day care facility.

My mother would climb into the dumpster in the back of this Giant Eagle store and gather up anything she could. Fruits and vegetables that she could cut out the bad parts, dented cans, opened boxes of macaroni and cereal to feed the family!

I can remember standing in this long line at the borough building down by the railroad tracks with her to receive blocks of butter and cheese and these huge tubs of peanut butter!

That was welfare back then!

One night when I was about eight years old my mother discovered that I was missing from my bed; she went out into the night to look for me.

She found me sleep-walking in my bare feet wearing only my pajamas by the Coney Island hot dog restaurant two blocks away on Braddock Avenue. She told me all about it the next day but I never could remember a thing about it!

"Maybe I just wanted a hot dog!"

I Escaped the Grip of the Grim Reaper

My mother Josephine was a good and loving mom to all of us, and I'm sure it was a hard life for her raising us without a husband but she was also a very stern woman!

She would always tell people that she was a police officer but really she was just a school crossing guard and she also worked as the late shift police dispatcher for the borough of Braddock for many years.

Although I have never officially been arrested in my entire life I can remember getting into a couple of fist fights and once getting caught ripping out copper pipes from an abandoned house to sell at the scrap yard, a police officer would take me to the station in handcuffs.

As we walked past my mother working at her desk the officer would say, "I have your son here Josephine," she would ask,

"What the hell did he do this time?"

The officer would tell her and she would immediately say,

"Lock him up for the night!"

I wasn't a bad kid, just a little mischievous! But I never had to pay any fines or go to court for the few little things I got into trouble over,

"Thank you Mom!"

My mother's health began to fail in her late fifties; she would soon retire and move to Memphis, Tennessee and live with my sister Arlene until she died of a heart attack in 1992 at the age of sixty-three.

I quit high school in the tenth grade and joined the US Navy at the ripe age of seventeen just to get out of this ghetto and the racial conflicts caused by the assassination of Martin Luther King Jr. on April 4, 1968.

I served on a guided missile destroyer US naval ship during the Vietnam conflict as a loader of seventy-five pound five inch projectiles deep in the bottoms of the warship among other duties as a messenger from the Signal Bridge to the 'XO,' Executive Officer, or the second in command of the ship during 'General Quarters,' or Battle Stations!

While I was on this war ship on a West Pacific 'West Pac' military duty our ship along with another Destroyer went up some river on an assignment to destroy an ammunition depot, if I can remember correctly this was in August 1972.

During this 'Mission,' my ship received return fire in which I still have five photographs of explosions in the river taken from someone on the signal bridge that nearly hit our ship, but our mission was apparently successful! This was all confirmed by the memos posted on the bulletin the next day!

While on this campaign we would be on the shores of Viet Nam for two or three weeks at a time then go to the Philippine Islands, Hong Kong, Japan, and Kaohsiung, Taiwan, for 'Liberty,' or as a short vacation!

Our ship had three of these 'Liberties,' in the Philippine Islands, at the naval base Subic Bay.

Next to the base was Olongapo City in which it was later devastated on June 15, 1991 by a Mount Pinatubo volcano in which more than sixty people were killed, or so I read!

After the nine month tour of the Viet Nam campaign and on the night before my ship was set to return to our home port of San Diego, there was an incident that almost changed my young life forever and almost had me in a prison in the Philippines' for a long time.

I was sort of involved with a 'bar girl,' I would always meet up with her when I was in the Philippines, her name was Rebecca!

At about five o'clock in the afternoon I met up with Rebecca at the bar that she hung out at.

Soon she and her girlfriend, I don't quite remember her name, wanted to go to some house for a fix, in other words, to use heroin!

I went along; I stayed in the living room while the two women were shooting up in the bedroom.

An hour or so later at the bar as Rebecca, her girlfriend and I were dancing,

Rebecca's girlfriend collapsed onto the floor!

As a crowd gathered around her an ambulance was called, the ambulance didn't come in time, and this girl died right there on the dance floor!

I was not alone, I had five friends from my ship with me, they did not try to help me when three African American Marines surrounded me and pushed me into a corner.

One of them broke a beer bottle and put the broken edge to my throat accusing me of giving the women this heroin.

Then the Philippine police stepped in between us pushing the Marines away, and then the US Military Police came in the bar and got involved.

Soon most of the people left the bar including my friends. After nearly an hour of explaining that I had nothing to do with the whole thing and with

Rebecca crying and corroborating my story, she was then taken away by the police. I was then allowed to leave the bar but ordered to return to my ship by the MPs, or the Military Police!

What a night that was!

After I was discharged from the Navy I was employed as an auto body and fender repairman for years until I started buying homes in which I would then rent or sell them again for a profit and in the late 1990's I was also buying and selling at flea markets.

Chapter 2: My Bucket List!

I was sitting on the back deck of our North Carolina home in early December 2011, Marcia, 'my fiancée,' and I was cooking out with our grill preparing steaks!

I was just sitting there in the beautiful sun of the North Carolina winter thinking about how we didn't do this often enough. We brought this very nice grill down from Pittsburgh to our home we purchased way back in 2003, but we haven't used it in all of those past eight years, in fact we had to get the propane tank filled.

I was just sitting there thinking about how I let work control my life;

I just wasn't having fun anymore. I then thought about how I loved going to the public pools in the summers but I haven't done this for well over two years. It was then the winter season but not even in the nicer weather of North Carolina are the public pools open in December, so I thought I'd sign up for the local YMCA, something that I always thought I'd like to do some day but like I said, I worked all the time buying and fixing houses, and also doing the flea market thing.

I was also so cheap! I never joined!

I didn't realize it at the time but I was collecting a

"Bucket List,"

I thought we'd sell our home and move permanently back to Pittsburgh that year of 2012, Marcia and I originally thought we would sell it a year later in 2013, but why wait?

The flea market fire of September the third of 2010, at the Webb Road flea market in Salisbury, North Carolina in which Marcia and I were inside vendors left us with no real reason to stay in North Carolina any longer!

I was also thinking that when we got back to Pittsburgh the following spring, I'd look into getting something done about the deep wrinkles in my forehead;

I am not a particularly good looking man!

I wish I was, but we all can't be handsome, right?

Anyway, I had these two deep lines across my forehead caused by not so much age; they were more of worry lines or frown lines!

I used to worry about everything!

At this same time I was still finishing up a tell-all book on my computer about the flea market just mentioned that burned down! I was also looking into maybe going to Lake Norman, a huge man-made lake not far from our Salisbury home on the internet.

Marcia and I went to this lake for a day when her daughter Michelle and her boyfriend Tim came from Pittsburgh to visit one time a few years ago. Using my brand new chainsaw Tim and I cut down twenty or so trees and we all helped in burning the brush and then I had some logging company come to take the big timbers away for free.

"Those were some good times!"

When the four of us went to this lake only Tim and I brought swimming shorts, so when we found a part of the lake that had public swimming, I was thrilled! Tim and I went into the locker -room to change. We then went into the water. I didn't much care for it, the water was warm and the lakes in North Carolina are more of a brown color, and the shores are mud.

I did have some fun 'never the less'!

This one time Bobby, Marcia's son, and I went to Keystone, a state park some fifty miles south-east of Pittsburgh when I was there alone buying yet another house and while Marcia worked the flea market in North Carolina. Bobby and I swam in the lake for an hour or so, we then drove to the Conemaugh Dam camp grounds just a few miles away and watched as people were riding jet skis.

I liked the idea of doing it one day!

So, while I was writing my tell-all book I also looked into renting a cabin at this Lake Normon for a weekend. I soon called for details, and yes, there was a part of the beach that had Jet Ski rentals.

I talked to Marcia about it but she just doesn't like doing these kinds of things and she doesn't know how to swim any way!

She would say,

"Why can't you go by yourself?"

Damn, I didn't want to go alone!

"What kind of fun would that be?" That whole idea soon went by the waste side.

I Escaped the Grip of the Grim Reaper

I also thought about how I would love to see the 'Grand Canyon,' in Arizona someday before I die. I once watched on the Discovery channel about how this huge glass floored skywalk was erected to view the awesome canyon.

I also thought that I'd go to a 'Starbucks' and buy one of those famous $5.00 cups of coffee!Folks, here I was fifty-seven years old but I never had a cup of coffee at Starbucks.

These are the things I thought of while I was on the deck of our North Carolina home cooking out and since my father died at that same age of fifty seven, I felt that I better hurry up and start to live my life while I still had the chance.

I hardly remember my father except for him being a real thin man and being an alcoholic! My mother told me that when I was still in diapers my father had to go the Braddock Hospital to get stitches in his head because she hit him with the telephone as he was drunk and they got into an argument.

As a kid I was forbidden to talk to my father if I was ever to see him on the streets by my mother!

I mentioned that she was very stern! It wasn't until I was in my late twenties that I ever really talked to the man, where else?

But at a bar! I just happened to stop in for a quick beer and shoot a game of pool with a friend of mine, and there he was sitting at the end of the bar, he looked like a pitiful, broken man! He staggered as he came to me saying,

"Robert, I'm your father! Do you know that?" I answered,

"Yes, I know who you are!"

He then asked if I could buy him a beer, this man never supported me or my brothers and sister and he asks me to buy him a beer, but I did buy him one anyway.

We had not much to say other than that to each other. I heard he died soon after that.

I am a believer in the concept that people live as long as their parents, unless of course you die in some kind of accident, it's all in the Genes.

So again I just felt that I needed to start living my life and I better hurry.

Marcia and I soon finished our delicious steak and baked potato. She cleaned up and went into the house while I stayed outside for quite a while just enjoying the beautiful sun of the North Carolina December afternoon!

The very next morning after I had breakfast, I then immediately wrapped my swimming trunks with a bath towel and I drove to the J.F. Hurley family YMCA on Jake Alexander Street in Salisbury, North Carolina.

It's a beautiful facility; it has a full size Olympic swimming pool there and also a second warmer pool but shallow with a huge sliding board for the kids, I so much wanted to try it but I weighed 260 pounds.

"I didn't want to splash all of the water out!"

Right between the two pools you would find the greatest huge hot tub with many water jets!

Of course I joined, I stayed for nearly three hours going back and forth to the pools and to the hot tub that first day, I was mad at myself for not doing this sooner, I just loved it so much. I was to go every day except for one day over the next twelve days.

During this time I was drinking a lot of fruit juices, eating a lot of cake, ice cream, fruit cocktail right out of big cans and so forth to build up my stamina. I wanted to lose some weight. At least that's what I thought.

But on Saturday December 17, 2011 while I was home sleeping after three hours of swimming then coming home and eating a big piece of frozen orange icing cake and some vanilla ice cream, Marcia soon heard a loud thump as she was doing laundry, she came into the bedroom and saw me lying on the floor face down with my head less than an inch away from hitting my dresser, she cried out,

"Honey, are you alright?"

I gave no response; she then ran to the phone and called 911!

Incredibly the ambulance was there within five minutes, they came to me, tried to do 'CPR' on me by sticking a needle in my arm with adrenaline and pounding on my chest.

They told Marcia that they thought I was 'Dead'! They were wrong! They hurried me onto a stretcher and rushed me to the emergency room of the Rowan County hospital with Marcia following in her car.

From what I was told, I died on the way to the hospital. The staff there feverishly used those shock paddles on my chest until I had a very faint heartbeat; the doctors then connected me up with life support systems and a breathing tube.

I Escaped the Grip of the Grim Reaper

A doctor soon came into a waiting room to see my fiancée Marcia, he told her briefly about how I was probably going to die, and asked if we were married.

She told him we were not, and that we were only engaged!

He then asked if I had children. Marcia told him that I had a daughter but she was living in Pittsburgh. The doctor then asked if I had a living will, Marcia answered,

"No! I don't think so," Then he asked,

"Do you have a way of contacting his daughter?"

Marcia answered by saying that she had the get my daughter's phone number from my own personal phone book.

Marcia soon left the hospital fighting off her tears!

As she arrived at our home she immediately located my phone book and called the admissions desk of the hospital to tell them that my daughter's name was Mary, and then gave them her phone number.

Marcia; waited a while for the hospital to talk to Mary but apparently they weren't able to get in touch with her.

My daughter as many nowadays, does not answer her phone, especially when the call comes from my phone! So Marcia called again and again until she answered,

"Mary, its' Marcia, did the hospital down here call you?" Mary said,

"No Marcia they haven't, what's this all about?"

"Your dad's in the hospital," Marcia cried,

"What happened?" My daughter then asked,

"I'm not quite sure but they say he had some kind of sugar attack that shut down his pancreas and it caused him to have a heart attack and he's in real bad shape Mary," Marcia said as she sobbed,

My daughter soon received the phone call from the hospital and was told that I was probably going to die and that they needed her permission to turn off the life support systems, and that she had to come to the hospital to sign these papers in person.

My daughter agreed to drive to North Carolina, but it took a few days to make all of the arrangements for her mother-in law to baby sit her two children.

When Mary and her husband finally drove down they went straight to the hospital.

Marcia was there waiting for her. Marcia led Mary and her husband Mike where to go, soon after they all met up with the doctor.

The doctor told Mary of my prognosis saying I only had a twenty percent chance of living and even if I lived I'd most certainly have brain damage because I died for quite a few minutes, and didn't have oxygen to my brain.

My daughter and Marcia were standing over me with tears in their eyes!

Or so I was told!

My daughter then asked that they give me a couple of days, and give me a chance to live, the doctor disagreed with her but told my daughter they would.

The next day I was given a brain scan and it showed that my brain seemed to be okay; and then my heart was beginning to get stronger. My prognosis then changed to a fifty percent chance of living, but I was in a coma, a coma that lasted for twenty one days.

Chapter 3: My Recovery!

On January 8, 2012, a Sunday, my eyes finally opened, I was off of the life support systems and wheeled into an intensive care unit 'ICU'

My mind was still in a fog because I thought I was taken to the basement of my San Diego home.

First of all, I haven't lived in San Diego since 1973, I was a seaman in the US Navy then and I had my own apartment, but I had no basement!

I remember two male nurses picking me up and hoisted me up onto another bed. The bed was faced out to view the door and a large window with an opened drape so that I could look out into the hall. I can see another room and a small table in the hallway.

Another male nurse soon came into my room greeting me by saying,

"Hello Mr. Lee!"

He then stuck a few large red stars on my hospital gown, saying,

"Soon you will have enough of these stars to be released from the hospital!"

He then left my room. I was still groggy and I didn't say anything to this nurse, I was confused to say the least! I then looked down at my gown and there weren't any red stars on my gown. I guess I was still medicated or just plumb crazy, I didn't know which!

Then a lady nurse came into my room saying,

"Hello Mr. Lee, how are you?" I asked,

"Ok, I guess, but where am I?" She replied,

"You're at the Rowan County hospital!" I just uttered,

"Why?" the nurse then said,

"Mr. Lee, you got sick a few weeks ago and you were brought to the hospital," I then asked,

"What happened to me?" The nurse answered by saying,

"I personally don't know a lot, but you are one lucky man, everybody thought you would die, it had something to do with your pancreas!" Then she said,

"The doctor will be coming in soon to talk to you."

The nurse checked my blood pressure, she checked my heartbeat and my pulse then she stuck a needle in my right arm and another one in my belly and said,

"I'll see you later this afternoon."

I would later watch my beloved Pittsburgh Steelers lose to the Denver Broncos' 29-23 in overtime of the NFL Wildcard football Game, and in humor, I almost wished that I stayed in my coma an extra day so that I would have missed the game!

The next morning as I was just waking up, I was peering out into the hallway; a nurse was walking past my room,

She looked familiar! I sort of waved to her, she acknowledged me, she smiled but kept on walking by, I'm thinking,

"Where do I know her from?" I didn't really know anyone from there in Salisbury, and then I remembered she was in one of my 'delusions,' or dreams.

She was a nurse who lived in a house right next to a library for which I will talk about as I go along!

I'm sitting there with her in this kitchen, she was dressing for work and telling me that she was quitting her job soon at the hospital because she couldn't take the stress of seeing people sick and dying all of the time, this woman looked a lot like my daughter's mother Maria.

I was never to see this nurse again!

Perhaps she wasn't assigned to my care in any way, but how do I know her face? Did she talk to me while I was in a coma? Or, was she talking to someone else when she was in my room checking on me? Did I hear her even though I was in a coma? Did she quit her job like she said she was going to do? Is that why I never saw her again?

I don't know, I just don't know!

Soon breakfast was brought to me, pretty good, but just a small portion of scrambled eggs, one slice of toast, a small carton of apple juice and coffee, no sugar!

I watched some television, mostly the news shows. My vision was different, it felt like I had sleep in my eyes, I rubbed my eyes again and again but it didn't help, but by the next day my vision seemed to be alright. Later that second day in recovery a male nurse came into my room; I got real scared because I recognized him as a bad man in some of my delusions! He said,

"Hello, Mr. Lee," he said his name but I don't remember,

I Escaped the Grip of the Grim Reaper

"I need to check your blood pressure."

By now I was a little convinced that these were just delusions that I had, and I must have opened my eyes to know his face so I was ok with him, and I said,

"I know your face, you were in my delusions!" he chuckled,

"You were not a nice man!" I added.

"Well Mr. Lee, I hope to see you again and you could tell me all about what I did in your delusions."

I was never to see this male nurse again either!

This male nurse was in my delusions as a bad man in some of them. In one delusion he had my hands tied to the back of a chair and demanded that I tell him where I hid my money, he also demanded I give him my address so he could break in and steal my fiancée's jewelry. I eventually gave in to him but for only my money, telling him he'd have to kill me before I gave him our address.

In another delusion I saw this male nurse opening my checking account box and pulling out $7,000 in $100 bills. I don't remember ever telling him where this money was! Maybe I came out of the coma too soon to finish this particular delusion!

"Pretty damn wild don't you think?"

When I saw my fiancée for the first time I asked her if she still had her jewelry, she asked,

"What are you talking about, of course I do," I then told her about my delusion.

This same man was in another delusion, but this time he was helping me to investigate the murder of two slaves during the civil war. I knew just one name of the slaves, his name being Warren, that's all I knew. We were in the attic of my so called San Diego home, and again I will remind you that it was just an apartment, I had no attic. We were looking at photographs of these two slaves. I had what seemed to be a holster and hand gun that belonged to Warren, don't ask me why a slave would own a holster and a pistol,

It was only a delusion!

I talked personally to the owner of these two slaves at their plantation, the man and his son both denied killing them.

Marcia was also there with us in this attic; she was hemming the length of a pair of my jeans with a sewing machine, without saying a word.

In yet another delusion with this male nurse we both were sitting in a room waiting to be seen by a doctor, I kept pulling off the little temperature sensor from my finger, 'I think that is what it was', and he kept saying,

"Keep the thing on your finger or you will die!"

I would not listen; I just kept taking it off.

In another delusion with him, he was on my ship with me back in 1973, and he injected poison into someone who was complaining that the ship had no walls, can you believe it? A ship without walls, wouldn't the ship sink?

Am I just crazy? I also saw myself at a Starbucks, perhaps because going there was on my bucket list, but this was no ordinary Starbucks, it was on the top floor of a tall white stone public library,

"No drive thru!"

I was sitting in a wheel-chair in a hall way by the door looking inside, I had these blue socks on with those non-slip pads on the bottom, my feet were hot and itchy, but when I reached to pull them off, the socks were glued to my feet!

I was then on another floor of this tall white library looking for information about historical black people of the nine-teenth century and dropping books down a tube on the floor to the first floor but into a wet grassy area as it was raining, I saw myself picking up these books with my wet hair, one of these books was about Frederick Douglass, an abolitionist of slavery born in 1818.

I also saw my daughter in one delusion; she was sitting on a Penny-farthing bicycle, on a hilly street, in the rain!

There are a couple of things that amuse me about this delusion, I had to look up this bicycle for one thing on the internet for I didn't know what a big front wheeled bicycle was and another thing is the 'rain', it seems that there was rain in quite a few of my delusions.

Was it raining often when I was in the coma and was I near a window while I was in the coma?

Anyway, her hair was soaking wet, and her face was real shinny and wet and she said,

"Daddy don't worry, you'll be ok!"

I then saw four nurses standing around my hospital bed, Although they had those old type of nurse caps on that they would wear when I was a kid, they were also wearing Dallas Cowboy cheerleader outfits, I was trying

I Escaped the Grip of the Grim Reaper

to get these nurses fired because I felt them to be lazy and incompetent. In this same delusion as I was lying there, I said to one of them,

"Honey, I'm not going to die!" I laughed when I said it, but I meant it, then I added,

"How about a shot of Southern Comfort?"

I don't even drink except when I go to a bar that has Karaoke. Yes I sing, I'm real good at it too, people call me Bobby Lee. I sing, 'Kentucky Rain' and 'Suspicious Minds' by Elvis Presley, and I might sing the best ever rendition of 'Turn the Page' by Bob Seger, I also sing many other songs.

In one delusion, don't worry! I'm almost done, I almost forgot this one. I was standing in a long line of patients to have my brain operated on!

I cut the line to get to the front because I was in a hurry to make an appointment for I was a politician running for some kind of office for which I could never figure out, but I do know I was a 'Republican,'

Is that crazy or what?

I remember after cutting the line I was lying on a green carpet in some office type room on my back with my brain bouncing from ear to ear, and remember saying to the surgeon,

"A little to the right please!" and then thanking him for letting me cut the line.

In one last delusion I will tell you of; there were plenty more! I saw myself sitting in my recliner at my North Carolina home again as the rain pelted on the window next to me, when Santa Claus came out of our fireplace, and we didn't even have a fireplace!

He was sort of vibrating and he was also Japanese! Again these were just a few of my delusions.

I do admit that when I was in my teen age years I flirted with LSD a few times, just a few times folks!

But these delusions felt so real.

Ever since this happened, people would ask me if I saw lights at the end of a tunnel, or if I had an,

"Out of the body spiritual experience?"

I honestly don't remember, I never much believed in any sort of God, but often through the years I would pray to him,

Just in case!

I was then transferred to another nicer more private room on the second floor later that night, maybe that's why I never saw the lady or the male nurse again! Who knows?

After five days in my private room I thought I was going to be released from the hospital on the Friday of the Martin Luther King Jr. holiday. My doctor came in my room, this turned out to be the first and only time I met him. He said,

"Hello, I'm Doctor Singh, how are you?"

He then sat in a chair and first asked my name and my social security number as he was looking at some papers,

I answered the questions. He then said,

"Mr. Lee you are one incredible man,"

I asked,

"What happened to me?" he answered,

"You had a sugar attack or pancreatitis!" I interrupted the doctor to ask if I had diabetes, he answered,

"No, you don't have diabetes but do you drink alcohol?"

I told him that I rarely drink and then told him my shortened story of how I was eating and drinking a lot of sugary things since I joined the YMCA to build up my stamina. The doctor then said,

"This must have caused your pancreas to fail and that gave you a heart attack and shut down all of your other organs, but now you are just fine. We mended your pancreas, your liver is fine and your kidneys are fine, even your heart is in great shape."

I then asked about my lungs, he said,

"They are fine as well."

"Then I can smoke again!" I laughed.

The doctor said that was up to me, he then said that it was a weekend and that he'd like to keep me there for another couple of days and I would be discharged on that coming Monday, Martin Luther King Day.

I didn't want to argue with the man that saved my life so I said that would be fine. I thanked the doctor and he soon left my room.

To this day I am still confused! How in the hell could sugar kill me? I didn't know that I was hurting myself! I don't have diabetes; it's not even something that runs in my family!

We all die from heart attacks!

I Escaped the Grip of the Grim Reaper

I can remember having the worst case of 'mud mouth,' during this time. I guess I was suffering from dehydration and drinking Pepsi, Ginger ale, and an assortment of fruit juices was the only things that were helping.

I totally lost my taste for meat and chicken except for an occasional trip to Taco Bell for a taco or burrito after I went swimming at the YMCA. I was basically eating pure sugar, but I felt great, I had no warning, I even went out of my ordinary routine of eating cereals like Rice Chex, Total and corn flakes, but then one day when Marcia went shopping I asked her to buy me Co Co Puffs and Trix, both having a high content of sugar.

Wow, I just can't imagine how I let this happen!

A physical therapist came in my room later that same morning and for the first time I stood up and with the aid of a walker struggled into the bathroom and moved my bowels,

"No more crapping in a bed pan for me!"

Over the weekend I of course watched the other football games since the Steelers were out of contention which still pisses me off!

When that Monday finally came I woke up with excitement for I was soon going home!

As that morning passed by, it looked like I wasn't going to be released after all that day either.

But at about one o'clock in the afternoon a woman came in my room saying,

"Mr. Lee, are you Robert Lee?" I answered,

"Yes ma'am!"

"Sir, I'm Ms. Johnson, I'm a psychiatrist with the hospital and I'd like talk to you."

I already knew I was going to be seeing a psychiatrist because they said I didn't have oxygen to my brain when I died for those few minutes, but I knew I was fine, and so did all of the nurses and doctors, but I guess I still had to be tested.

She first asked me the social security number thing,

Then she sat in the chair in front of me, she read a short little story then she showed me a drawing for a minute. We then talked about what happened to me, I told her of the delusions I had, she smiled saying the delusions were probably a result of the medications that were used.

After about five minutes, she asked if I could repeat the short story she read to me, I replied,

"On March the third 1989, in Cleveland, Ohio a three alarm fire broke out in two warehouses, one warehouse was completely destroyed but the other one was saved."

"Mr. Lee you read that perfectly, now will you draw that figure I showed you?"

She handed me a piece of blank white paper on a clipboard and a pencil, I drew a somewhat perfect free hand rectangle, I drew a half circle on the right side, then I drew an X to all four corners and then I drew three little circles in the left side corner and gave it back to her,

"You passed sir, there sure isn't anything wrong with your mind, I will sign your discharge papers, take care now, goodbye!"

I was soon released that day finally, exactly thirty days after I first died, I was going home. A hospital custodian wheeled me up to the third floor exit on the elevator.

The driver of this big hospital van then strapped me with the wheel chair to the floor of the hydraulic lift and soon I was on my way home.

It was good to see the sun again although it was a little chilly by now in January; the travel time was a good forty minutes.

I was feeling a lot of joy!

Chapter 4: Home at Last!

I was finally at my North Carolina home. I was so happy to be with Marcia and my three cats, all 'B' named, Baby, Bootsy, and my Buffy. I say my Buffy because I found her in a shed where I stored my rider lawn mower at one of my rental homes in Pittsburgh, I had so much trouble grabbing her as she kept darting from me. I opened a can of evaporated milk for her and placed a bowl of it on the steps leading up to the back porch, I was finally able to grab this all dark grey kitten with the smallest white patch on the front of her neck.

A friend later told me that she was a pedigree, a Russian Blue. It took some time to bond with her, I loved her so much! I say loved in the past tense because I would eventually lose her, I will write of this later.

As I sat in my recliner just relaxing, Marcia came to me with a kiss and said,

"Welcome home!"

Marcia then made me a great meal of baked chicken, mashed potatoes and sweet peas.

Soon after dinner I asked Marcia to roll me a few cigarettes, yes! I'm sorry but I decided I would smoke again.

Marcia and I no longer buy conventional cigarettes, we now roll our own. We bought a pretty neat machine that you put your tobacco in and crank it and 'Walla,' you have a cigarette. Easy, once you get the hang of it, and so much cheaper, too.

I smoked my first cigarette in five weeks, I should have quit, I had the best chance then of doing so!

I later watched some television using my own remote, the remote for my television at the hospital really sucked!

It was a big and awkward thing and it was connected to the functions of the bed and to the nurse out in the huge lobby.

A few times I accidentally called the nurse for assistance.

I soon struggled with my walker into our bedroom and fell asleep. The next morning after having a breakfast of bacon, eggs and one slice of toast, Marcia and I had a long conversation. It was so nice to talk to her again. We must have talked for three hours with me doing the most talking, Marcia being the quiet type!

I told her that I had almost died once before years ago when a big van almost rolled over my stomach. She asked,

"How did that happen?"

I went on to tell her that back in 1995, I received a phone call from a dear old lady I once knew from the flea market. She called me saying that the drive shaft on her van was making a banging noise and she was afraid to drive it home from the flea market, and then asked if I could possibly look at it.

I told Caroline that the nuts and bolts on the universal joints probably got loose.

Universal joints allow the drive shaft to spin then that allows the rear wheels to spin. Most vehicles today don't use drive shafts or universal joints, because they are for the most part front wheel drive vehicles.

I told Caroline that I may be able to tighten the nuts and that I'd be right over, I grabbed a tool box with the tools that I would need and drove to the flea market.

After a quick greeting with Caroline I crawled under the van, plenty of room under the older vans. I saw that the universal joint connecting the drive shaft to the rear end axle was busted up pretty bad. I told her that I'd have to remove it, and go to a parts store to get a new one.

She said,

"That will be fine! I'll give you the money,"

I crawled back out from under the van and found a ratchet a few sockets and a few wrenches out of my tool box and crawled back under the van.

The van seemed to be on a flat asphalt surface but when I freed up the old universal joint the van began to roll, I shouted out,

"Put the emergency brake on!"

Because of the height under the van I was able to hold onto the frame and the rear axle as I was trying to walk along with my feet trying to keep the van from rolling over my then skinny stomach!

The dear old lady was frantic I'm sure, but she was able to get into the moving van and stop it, saving my life! She climbed back out of the van crying out,

"Are you alright?"

I Escaped the Grip of the Grim Reaper

This happened on a chilly day in early October of that year so I was wearing a heavy sweat shirt which probably helped.

But my back was still messed up, serious brush burns that would require ointments and Vaseline for weeks and even today there are fine visible scars,

But I still finished the job!

I went straight to the parts store; with my burning back, got the part, ad drove back to the flea market.

I then crawled back under the van and replaced the universal joint!

Caroline then told me to go straight home and that she would stop at a drug store to get a tube of anti-bacterial ointment and she'd come to my house to rub some on my back.

This is what I get for being a nice guy!

How stupid of me not to put the emergency brake on and blocking the wheels, and the poor old lady since deceased, must have thought about the horror of this for all of her last years. I most certainly escaped the grip of the Grim Reaper back then too!

Marcia asked why I never told her of this, I replied,

"I didn't want you to know how stupid I was!"

Soon after I told Marcia this horror story, she served me a small plate of lasagna and a toasted slice of garlic bread. Later in the afternoon I looked over a stack of bills that Marcia paid while I was in the hospital.

I then looked at my bank statement to check on my rental incomes, I had my tenants deposit their rents by using my bank account number while I was in North Carolina. I then called my bank's 1-800 line to get my most present balance. When I heard that my balance was only a little over $2,000 I thought that it couldn't be right, so I chose to hear recent withdrawals on the menu. When I heard that there was a cash withdrawal of $5,000 on January 13, 2012.

I about flipped out!

I called the main office and found out that my daughter Mary withdrew the money. I asked the bank manager how she was able to do this further stating that she was not even on my account,

"She is now!"

The bank manager went on telling me that she had a legal document saying that she was now my guardian! Of course I was flabbergasted and angry.

I called my wonderful daughter, and got her voice mail,

"Mary, it appears that you took money out of my account, call your father,"

I called several times and I got angrier as she would not answer her phone, I finally got her to answer her phone,

"You **** bitch! Why did you take my money out of my account?"

She put her husband on the phone and we went at it, he kept saying bullshit like that I should thank my daughter for saving my life and that I owed her, and I should be glad that she didn't take out the whole $7,500 that I had in the account. He then said they drove all the way to North Carolina and paid Mary's mother to baby sit her two kids.

I demanded,

"That cost $5,000?"

The fighting over the phone continued for the next few days, I told him I would call my attorney. He said that if I did that it would cost me more in the end. I of course told him that we would see about that. I did call my attorney and at this date the lawsuit is still going on and I will win, I always win, right is right, this was criminal!

She knew I was supposed to get out of the hospital on January 13, because I told her so in the one and only conversation I had with her a few days before I was released, and she knew I was 'competent,' just by talking to her, but she ran to my bank up in Pittsburgh with this document and told them that I was incompetent to pay my bills, do you believe this shit?

I will have satisfaction in the end! She never paid any of my bills.

Mary and her husband own a $140,000 home with a huge in-ground swimming pool, and the both of them drive nice cars. They stole my money. The wheels of justice turn slow, but they do turn!

Chapter 5: My loving daughter!

Sometime in June of some year, I don't even care to write it in at this moment, this daughter of mine was born out of wedlock with myself as the father, and Maria as her mother.

Maria and I had a good relationship for the first few years, but eventually it fell apart, but we had a beautiful little girl, we named her Mary! She was just the normal kid growing up; 'spoiled,' between her mother and I, we really spoiled her.

Every Christmas, and every Birthday I would buy her the latest Barbie and Ken dolls, she kept them in their un-opened boxes, I built a whole wall of shelves in her bedroom to show off the thirty or more of them.

One day when she was sixteen or so, again I choose not to remember, a friend and Mary took them all to the flea market and sold them for a small fraction of what I paid for them! I didn't even know about this until I helped her and her husband move into their new home, I asked in curiosity,

"Mary, where are all of your Barbie Dolls?"

That's when I found out!

As she entered her teens I'd take her to JC Penneys, the Old Navy store and I'd spend $700 for her school clothes every year. When she was sixteen she made the mistake of telling me she was in home schooling, I asked her why she let me buy her new school clothes that year; she replied,

"I still needed new clothes Daddy!"

This one time I'll never forget, we were at my house, she was I'd say twelve years old, as we left the house and walked to my car, I could see that she was hiding something under her coat. I asked,

"What do you have under your coat?"

I went to her and she handed me a pile of my old and expensive super hero comic books, I was shocked,

"Why would you steal from me?"

"I need money Daddy," she cried.I then yelled,

"I always give you money,"

I took them back into the house and I took her home. I was mad, but I got over it.

As she got older I would take her out to eat and she would always order the most expensive dishes, and desserts on the menu, then she would only eat half of the food. She just loved me to spend money on her. I would even give her $50 or more, it would become a joke,

"Mary, every time I see you it costs me $100!"

When I met Marcia in 2001, Mary was maybe fifteen, she never liked Marcia. She just never gave her a chance. I think she felt threatened by Marcia in some way, perhaps because Marcia was un-like most of the women that I would date, she had class. Then Mary started dropping lines on me,

"Are you going to leave me money when you die?"

On the sixteen day of October 1995, a date that still lives in infamy with me, just three days after the time of the dear old lady and her universal joint problem in which I was almost killed, I found $19,000 in the kitchen Lazy Susan cabinet of my home that I had recently purchased.

I will talk in great detail about this again later in Chapter 11, Giving Back!

I immediately gave my daughter $1,000 even though Christmas wasn't for another two months. I even bought her mother two used cars over the next two years for a total of $4,000 even though I wasn't even dating her anymore. Mary was just nine years of age at this time, from then until she was seventeen I gave her $1,000 every Christmas.

When she turned eighteen and was already engaged, I figured the times of giving her $1,000 were over so I wrote her a check for only $750. I put it in an envelope and put in her mail box because she wasn't home when I went to give it to her.

On that very same evening while Marcia and I were having a beautiful Thanksgiving dinner at a friend's home she called my cell phone!

She demanded that I give her the extra money, she cried,

"Daddy you don't understand, I have all these gifts to buy for my family and friends all figured out, and I really need the money that you always gave me!"

She called four times until I shut off my phone.

I should have told her to put, 'From Robert Lee' on the gifts!

I never gave her the extra money!

I Escaped the Grip of the Grim Reaper

When she was preparing for her wedding with Mike, by the way a much older man by fifteen years, she asked me for $5,000 or should I say again demanded the money. I honestly didn't have it, I tried to negotiate with her, but there was no such thing with her. This was in 2004, at that time I only had two rentals, I was paying hospital bills of a neck surgery that you will read about later and I was paying off an old school loan.

I was also then and to this day I am still paying a court ordered debt in the amount of $14,000 to the Pennsylvania Department of Welfare for arrears of support that I never got credit for because Mary's mother was on welfare for most of my daughter's childhood, by the way it's just about paid off!

Needless to say I wasn't invited to her wedding. Oh, she did give me a DVD of her wedding a couple of years later,

"Yeah, I'm going to watch her wedding on DVD, Right!"

I just recently threw the damn thing away!

Recently back in October of 2011, when we were so called 'getting along,' I called her one evening, not that I called often; she answers,

"I'm watching a movie with my husband!" Then she hangs up on me.

When she drove to North Carolina to 'save my life,' I actually think that when she asked my doctors to give me a chance to live she believed I was going to die anyway, and she was going to get my houses and everything else I owned, she was just posturing, making herself look like the loving daughter she was impersonating.

One might call my daughter an opportunist, a year or so after she and Mike were living in their $140,000 house she discovered that it had some termites, she was able to sue the old owner for $20,000. I don't think she ever hired a professional to take care of them, and if I know Mary, she probably planted the termites! She also wanted to sue a Target department store because the concrete slabs by the entrance were slightly un-even and when Mary pushed her shopping cart over it, the cart shook and it made her baby cry.

Chapter 6: A time of reckoning!

On January 26, 2012, ten days after I was released from the hospital, I'm lying in my recliner, at this time I'm asking myself why in the hell didn't I just die? I was miserable; I had to use that stupid walker to get around. The two physical therapists that came to our home each week, both said it would be six to nine weeks before I could walk without it. I thought it would even take longer since I haven't done a damn thing to speed up the process of getting my legs back.

I was pissing in a glass and dumping the urine into a bigger container for Marcia to empty into the toilet, I was 197 pounds and still losing weight, I lost my appetite. Marcia would prepare good healthy small meals and I would only eat half of the meal.

As I sat in my recliner with my feet in an upward position, I noticed the nail on my big toe on my left foot wasn't completely brown any more, it was growing in white.

Twenty- five or so years ago, I was trying to hang a large heavy old wood framed mirror on my bedroom wall at a house that I owned back then, it was very heavy, the weight pulled the screw out of the wall and the mirror fell on my toe.

If you can remember cartoons when a characters thumb was smashed with a hammer, the characters thumb would swell and pulsate; this is what I thought of. With each heart beat it would send excruciating pain to my toe. This happened three or so in the morning so I didn't want to scream.

The next day this toe was black and the nail fell off, the new nail grew in brown and stayed brown all of these years. I would see these Lamisil commercials with these little critters climbing under a toe nail to get in, I had a fungus. I thought about buying the product but when I saw that there were so many possible side effects, I figured I'd just live with the brown toe. I once cut and dug out as much of the toe nail as I could and soaked my foot in bleach and vinegar for days, but my toe nail still grew in brown.

Now it's growing in as white as the rest of my toe nails.

I then noticed that the back of my neck wasn't itchy any more, and it hasn't been itchy since I died, so I felt the back of my neck, Ididn't have these little bumps any more, or should I say hives. My VA doctor referred this condition as 'urticaria.'

In 2001 shortly after the 911 terrorist attacks on our nation, Marcia and I purchased a home while still living in the Pittsburgh area, not our dream home so to speak, just another soon to be rental property, when someday soon we would be living in North Carolina!

We actually closed on the purchase on October 31st on Halloween, but it needed a lot of work. The first major job in the house was tearing down the ceilings in the upstairs bedrooms, the old plaster was literally falling down and I wanted a new look of a 'vaulted' ceiling with skylights.

This job required me nailing new 'two-by-four' boards in between the old supports which were old and very hard, I nailed so many boards in that my right arm would become limp, and the total job took almost whole month.

At this same time I was getting ready to put a new furnace in the home that we moved from, for my new tenant

But I had a real problem though!

I was feeling a lot of pain in my neck; also the two small fingers on my right hand had become numb after I pounded all of those nails.

I also suffered a neck injury way back in 1985 while simply putting a long extension ladder back on the bed rack of a truck owned by a friend of mine that did some roof work for me on an entirely different rental home I once owned.

I tried to jump with the ladder to get it on the rack and my neck snapped, even my friend Paul heard my neck snap from the front of the truck. I never had surgery but through physical therapy and two months of pain, my neck eventually got better!

At the time I didn't know why I was in so much pain, was it the pounding of the nails or did the injury of loading the ladder back in 1985 resurface.

I was so worried that I wouldn't be able to work on our new house and install the new furnace at the old house that I developed these hives.

Imagine worrying about not being able to work, most people would welcome a situation where they couldn't work for a while.

I Escaped the Grip of the Grim Reaper

I never got rid of them, I learned on the internet that rubbing the hives with vinegar would help the itching but I still never got rid of them, but now they're gone. I guess they're gone now because I was in la la land when I was in that coma and on all of the medication. I didn't worry about anything!

And about my toe growing in white, I think that may be due to not eating any processed foods for that time of also being in a coma.

Since I was then having this pain in my neck I thought I'd call Mike, a friend of mine in the heating and cooling business about him installing the new furnace for me.

I called Mike's cell phone only to learn that he was in Florida enjoying his retirement.

He suggested that I call the office and that his son could help me, for which I did call and made an appointment for Mike's son to come to the home and give me a price.

Two days later this heavy set young man without a speck of dirt on his hands, and not looking much like a working man shows up at the home,

I took him down to the basement to show him the furnace; he eventually gives me a 'special,' as he put it, price since I was an old friend of his father's for $4,000.

He even went as far as saying it had to be paid in 'green cash' since he was giving such a great deal.

I should add that the furnace didn't have central air conditioning so that wasn't a factor but I guess that wasn't too bad of a price back in 2002!

"But, not for me!" I told him that I would get back to him.

I instead called a local plumbing and heating company and got my own furnace and all of the parts I needed for $900, and installed it myself!

It took only three total days to finish the entire job,

How about that?

I'd like to point out, it's been ten years, I still own and rent the home and the new furnace is still working just fine!

After this furnace job, I just couldn't take the pain anymore! I soon had an operation on my neck in which a doctor cut the front of my throat and replaced three bones in the back of my neck using cadaver bones. The hospital stay was seven long days. I had to wear a neck brace and the surgeon told me to leave it on for six weeks never to take it off, not even to shower!

Well, the pain persisted! Then on another appointment the doctor said I'd have to have metal rods put in my neck.

I surely did not want metal rods in my neck!

I then decided to make an appointment for a second opinion, this time at the VA hospital to have another orthopedic doctor look at me.

Wearing my hard collar neck brace and after talking about the pain I still had, this Asian American doctor made an appointment for me to have some kind of nerve test but it wasn't scheduled for another three weeks.

Being the person I was, while I waited for the nerve test and while I was in my neck brace I then called the plumbing and heating company again and bought another furnace for our new home, tore out our old huge furnace, and with the help of Marcia we loaded it all in my big Dodge van and took it to the scrap yard. I then installed another new and more efficient furnace in our own home! Again,

How about that?

Even in a neck brace I refused to wait and do nothing!

I then finally had the nerve test done at the VA hospital.

God, the stinging pain was awful!

A nurse stuck these long needles in both of my arms over and over again as she went into another room, I guess to read and diagnose the readings.

Then yet another appointment was made for me to see the orthopedic doctor again.

When I saw this young Asian doctor again he drew a line on the inside part of my right elbow with a magic marker saying,

"This is where your problem is," then he asked,

"What kind of work do you do? Your ulner nerve is thin as a pencil lead, and the muscles around the nerve are compressing your nerve sending pain to your neck!"

I told him of all the work I had been doing, including the pounding of nails into the old roof supports which I think probably caused the whole problem.

I soon had that taken care of. I was only given a local anesthesia, the surgeon put the eight inch incision on the side of my elbow, he stitched my muscles away from the nerve inside and then stitched the outer skin back together, I can't recall the number of stitches needed but I'd say perhaps twenty.

The procedure took only twenty minutes and I was already painless. I had no pain what so ever in my neck anymore, but to this day I often have spasms in my neck and when they happen I just stand very still and relax until they pass!

And sometimes it feels like one of the cadaver bones pop a little out of place, I then just simply push it back in place, perhaps all of this will bite me on the ass one day and I will have to have more surgery!

Who knows?

I was also given a neat little battery operated electronic gizmo called a 'ten's unit,' that when I stick these little pads on with wires, it sends electrical shock waves to the muscles of my neck. This generates better blood flow to the cells or so I was told! I also use this on my chronic lower back problem too.

After I realized that my hives were gone and that my big toe wasn't brown anymore I began to think that dying and coming back to life wasn't so bad after all. I was now re-energized; I then thought that the physical therapists might be wrong about the time it would take for me to walk again by myself.

Perhaps they follow some kind of statistic of a man of my age, they didn't know of my determination or that I was a working man and that the calves of my legs were as hard as rocks before this all happened.

I also realized that I felt somehow smarter now, as I watched television, I thought a little deeper about the events transpiring, I remembered watching my cat Buffy trying to decide whether she would leave my bedroom or stay while I opened the door to go in the kitchen. I stood there with my walker and really got into her brain as she looked out into the kitchen then back at me in the bedroom, over and over again.

She knew she wouldn't get back into the bedroom for I would shut the door behind me, when it was cold we used electric baseboard heat but only heated the bedroom and living room during the night.

I was telling Marcia of these discoveries as she sat at the kitchen table cutting coupons, I then said,

"You know, I finished that stupid book about that stupid flea market! But I never believed in it, I felt it to be written well but who in the hell would buy it?"

Flea market sellers don't generally read books, and how about flea market buyers? Some of them might buy the book but not many! There just wouldn't be a great market for the book.

I then asked Marcia,

"What if I was to write a new book about what happened to me?"

She answered loudly,

"Yes, that would be a great book!" I then said,

"It's funny but I never thought to do so!"

I was excited!

I started to write my new book on paper with an ink pen, I'm not much of a computer 'geek,' and I didn't feel like typing at the moment. Once I started I couldn't stop, I couldn't sleep, for the next fifty-two hours I wrote, taking breaks to try to sleep, eating and going to the bathroom.

I finally told Marcia as she woke and came into the kitchen one morning,

"Honey you have to take me to the VA hospital," she asked,

"Why?"

I told her that I couldn't sleep and I might suffer some kind of brain damage if I don't soon get some sleep.

Soon with her driving we went to the hospital, it just happened to be a Sunday so the hospital was really under staffed, I had to check in, answer a bunch of questions, but after five hours I was finally given a bottle containing thirty sleeping pills.

But in hindsight I should have just gone to Walmart for Unisom or another over the counter sleeping aid, that's how weak these sleeping pills were, I took all thirty in five days! That's the VA health care system for you!

I'm just kidding really! The VA health care system has been good to me for many years!

All doctors today have to be careful about Prescription drug abuse!

I will write a lot about the different homes I have owned, this is important because with each home arises yet another story to tell, so please don't get too confused. I unfortunately have owned at one time or another nearly twenty of them! And trust me, I'm not bragging, I'm just stating facts.

I Escaped the Grip of the Grim Reaper

As a matter of fact I might as well tell you my story of how I got into this whole house buying and renting thing got started in the first place.

On February 28, 1983 Lorraine, my girlfriend back then was watching the very last episode of the famed Mash series about the Korean war and the care of injured soldiers starring Alan Alda as Hawkeye Pierce.

As she was laying on the couch in the living room a car suddenly came crashing in throwing the couch and Lorraine across the room, it was a miracle that she wasn't killed, only a few bumps and bruises. I was at the time sleeping in our bedroom on the second floor. The crash woke me up of course, I came running downstairs to see our living room full of smoke but thankfully no fire, and a stunned Lorraine screaming and crying.

I climbed over the couch to get to the car, which was halfway in the house and halfway hanging outside. I opened the door, reached past the slumped over driver and shut the ignition off! In the next few minute's police, ambulances, and fire trucks were all at the scene and in our home, apparently our next door neighbor called 911.The driver died in the crash, we were soon told that he was drunk, and driving too fast, he lost control and went airborne through our yard and into our house!

"How's that for a story?" I almost forgot about this event, actually it's the last story entered in the book!

As I said this was 1983; we only rented this home and we were obviously forced to find somewhere else to live and soon after that I bought my first home of my own!

Chapter 7: Marcia leaves me!

I first met Marcia at a bar that had Karaoke. The owner of the bar 'Fred' sort of fixed us up, this man Fred and his wife Caroline were friends of Marcia for many years in the flea market business. When Fred first leased this bar in June of 2001, Marcia not really into the drinking thing would go just to support Fred's new venture, one drink would last her for hours!

With Marcia having lost her husband the previous year to diabetes, her going to the bar was just a way to get out of the house and also a way of preventing her from being asked to baby sit her grand-children all of the time. I also knew Fred for a long time and was always telling him how sick and tired I was of the kind of girls I'd find myself with, 'bar flies.'

Marcia and I were both flea market vendors but at different markets in 2001 so we never met until Fred opened his bar!

We were just beginning our relationship at the time of the September 11th terrorist attacks against our nation. She called me that very morning to tell me to turn on my television. I'll never forget that tragic day! I am still so saddened by what happened that I still cry every year when the media has the anniversary shows.

Marcia and I drove to Shanksville Pa. a few weeks after that day to see the temporary memorial of Flight 93 in which I sobbed, I am an emotional type!

Soon after Marcia and I became an item, so to speak, I told her of my long-time desire to move to a warmer climate. I just dreaded the long, cold winters of Pittsburgh. Marcia liked the idea too.

I guess I was attracted to her by finally finding someone with the same goals that I had. Over the years I had a lot of girlfriends but Marcia was different, she had class, she owned a nice home in a family division called 'Camelot,' Located in North Huntington Pa.

This one time Fred was having a Hawaiian style party at his bar, this girl, a bar fly that I once had my turn with, I don't remember her name nor do I wish to at this moment, came to our table, I said,

"Hi, how are you?" and introduced her to Marcia,

This girl bends over squeezing on her breasts with her arms exposing her cleavage,

"You choose her over these?"

I just laughed and said,

"I sure do!"

Eventually after three years we found ourselves in Salisbury, North Carolina. We started to sell at the Webb Road flea market in October of 2006, and did well until that fateful day of September 3, 2010, the Friday of the Labor Day weekend, when it burned to the ground.

Marcia and I were devastated to say the least. We lost nearly $100,000 of super hero comics, vinyl records, collectable VHS movies, and DVDs. When I heard of all of the details of negligence and learned that it had no fire codes because it was built and deeded as a warehouse, I never wanted to be a part of it when the owners re-built the damn thing.

Marcia and I had a great relationship for the first ten years until she somehow changed after that flea market fire. We still owned our home there but we locked it up the following spring and came back up to Pittsburgh together, our relationship has gone downhill since. I thought that Marcia and I would be a team again; we bought a home in a small town called Donora.

We got it real cheap and it was loaded with a lot of nice furniture especially two beautiful bedroom suits and a brand new Maytag washer and dryer, the old owner inherited the home from her mother when she died but she lived in Georgia and didn't want to bother with the home or the furniture.

Marcia then began arguing with everything I would ask her to do, and that wasn't much, just paint for me, cleanup after me and to find things for me.

We would only work three or four hours a day on the Donora home. While I was on the floor putting baseboard moldings on, this one time, I asked her to get the other box of finishing nails from the very nextroom, she yelled out,

"I'm sweeping," I said loudly,

"So, I'm on the damn floor, please go and get them!"

She threw the broom against the wall and went and got them, another similar incident she, when asked to do something for me yelled out,

"You're not my boss!"

I yelled out,

I Escaped the Grip of the Grim Reaper

"I am your boss!"

There were more of these incidents, like when Marcia and I went to one of my rentals to cut the grass, this rental had a huge, maybe a half of an acre to cut with my rider-mower, I asked her to momentarily stop raking the fresh cut grass while she was smoking a cigarette to sweep the little bit of grass on the street because I had a real ass of a neighbor and I felt that it should be swept right away. I would have done it myself but I was using the weed-eater, just another chore I had to do because Marcia never wanted to learn how to use a gas powered weed eater! She threw the rake to the ground and yelled out,

"You're not my master!"

To this day I am still mad at her over these incidents! I am not a demanding person, no way!

I became afraid to ask her to do anything even to the point of going to work on my properties by myself. Was she just getting older and couldn't handle it any more or was it something else? Was it her daughters doing?

I never got along with her daughter or her husband Mark.

I moved completely out of my area into Marks area of Washington County because we often talked about buying homes together, and we would be a team! I had the financial means to buy houses and pay for the materials and he would do the work while I was in North Carolina.

Well this plan didn't work; I would soon learn how slow he worked because he liked to be on the computer all night long every night playing,

"Dungeons and Dragons," and internet gambling! I remember him saying,

"But it's so much fun!"

I eventually stopped calling him to work for me.

Now I'm stuck here today miles away from where I want to be, but enough of that for now!

Marcia's daughter Linda and her husband are jealous of anyone that may have more than they do and they do not like me or anybody else as a matter of fact.

I know that her daughter had been talking down on me to Marcia, about how I was buying homes without Marcia's name on the deeds. I bought these fixer upper homes from the money I received after selling my own home.

As far as me buying homes without Marcia's name on the deeds, she was in North Carolina working our rental space at the flea market for which I never asked for a dime of what she earned, while I was in Pittsburgh working on the homes. I didn't think it mattered! She never said anything about it.

I always expected that I would be with her until the day I died, we would have married but Marcia received death benefits from her late husband's social security and we thought she would lose those benefits.

This daughter of hers told Marcia that she didn't know why she put up with me; I know this to be true because it leaked down through another daughter to Marcia's son Bobby, who told me so.

Bobby and I are still great friends, I just had Easter Sunday dinner with him, his wife Janet and their two girls this past year, and they all still like me.

Marcia became more and more distant from me, we argued about everything!

I would ask for us to try to get along, she would agree and in the next few minutes the arguments would start again.

When I was sitting in my recliner all of the time because of my legs, I would wait for her to make me dinner, and wait, and wait! You can learn a lot about a person while you're disabled and sitting right there next to the kitchen. Marcia would be making me a meal and she would go to the bathroom, honestly she would be in there for twenty minutes every time.

Soon after Marcia and I met those years ago we went to a local Dairy Queen for ice cream, while eating my ice cream I had a case of 'Brain Freeze!'

Now I hope you folks know what that is? It's when you eat it too fast a nerve in your skull freezes and sends pain to the front of your brain, ergo 'Brain Freeze.'

The scientific name is Sphenopalatine Ganglioneuralgia,

"Wow, try pronouncing that!"

I asked Marcia,

"Don't you hate it when that happens?"

She replied,

"I wouldn't know! I never had it happen to me!"

You see; she does everything slow! That's why she never experienced this agonizing adventure of 'Brain freeze.'

Not that there's anything wrong with doing things slow, I guess she is just methodical in her actions and she will probably live into her late ninety's like her mother.

As for myself, I never had the luxury of doing things slow! I was always multi-tasking, although now, I am trying to take things just a little slower!

While I was home re-cooperating Marcia would argue with me that I had diabetes, I told her my doctor said I didn't, she would then ask,

"Then why are you taking insulin and checking your blood sugar with that meter?" I would answer,

"I don't know!"

Because I didn't know why at that time, I then asked the nurse the next time she came to our home, she said if I were to look at the label on the insulin bottle and the other medications I would see 'no refills,' she then said that the insulin and medicines were only to help in the healing of my pancreas, and not because I had diabetes!

Marcia would still go on about the fact that her husband died of diabetes, and he would go out and buy five candy bars at a time and hide them under the bed, and that was what killed him and if I didn't stop eating sugar the same thing would happen to me.

I would argue that I did cut down on my sugar, and she would argue back that I ate a container of ice cream in three days! I would say,

"Honey, the last container lasted almost a week," she'd answer,

"Bullshit!"

On February 7, 2012, the day after my fifty-eighth birthday, as I was again laying in my recliner when we got into an argument, Marcia stormed into the bedroom shutting the door behind her and I really let her have it, at this time I wasn't feeling so much like a new man with a better attitude.

I was feeling angry about the flea market burning down, I was angry that we now were forced to sell our home down in North Carolina, I was mad that I couldn't walk very well yet, angry with my daughter for having the audacity to steal $5,000 out of my bank account for saving my life.

I was still having trouble with my sleeping, when this episode happened I think I was up for thirty-five hours, yes, I had a lot of anger.

I started to scream at the top of my lungs,

"You are the stupidest person I have ever met." Then I yelled out,

"You are the slowest person I have ever met,"

Then I screamed out the loudest yet,

"Do you know why your husband would sneak those damn candy bars under the bed?"

I took a breath, and yelled again,

"So he could just die and get away from you!"

I must have rambled on for a good ten minutes until she cried, then she yelled from the bedroom,

"I'm leaving you!"

I yelled back,

"How soon?"

She said nothing else, later that evening she took the phone into the bedroom, when she came out she told me her step-son was coming down in three days to take her back to Pittsburgh. I just replied,

"The sooner, the better!"

The next morning I gave her our money market check book and told her that she could have all of the $19,800 in the account, I also told her that she could have all of the money we would get after we sell our North Carolina home! Since her daughter and her husband thought I was this evil monster.

I also asked that she not take my Buffy with her, she answered.

"She's your cat, of course I'll leave her here with you, but I'm taking Baby and Bootsy!"

I also wanted to make amends for getting Marcia into the whole selling her house and moving to North Carolina with me mess, in the first place! The night she left me she said she would call in a few days to see how I was doing! I guess she still cared for me being disabled and all.

Today I am ashamed of myself for yelling at her the way I did, I tried to get back with her a while after this horrible thing happened but I scarred her too deep, she is now living with her grand-daughter somewhere in a town not far from where I live named Charleroi, Pa.

Chapter 8: Still recovering but alone!

When Marcia left I was happy at first, it was three weeks since I got out of the hospital, I was getting around better but my legs were still sore. Often, I would get these burning sensations in my ribs and in my thighs; they felt like a cigarette burning inside my body!

I guess it was the medication I was taking that caused it or my blood circulation wasn't quite right yet, but soon these sensations ceased.

I soon learned that I could wash my dish's sitting down and fry an egg sitting down.

This one day I ran out of eggs, bread, coffee and a few other things, I asked myself,

"What am I going to do?"

I had this idea, I wasn't able to walk around the local Walmart to buy food yet, and I just wasn't ready for an adventure as demanding as that,

Walmart's are huge, and I didn't even think that I could have used one of those motorized carts that Walmart's have.

I made a detailed list of what I wanted. I drove to the Walmart with my still bad legs and with my walker went to a cashier and asked this pretty young lady to do my shopping, with a nice smile she said,

"Sure, I'd be happy to do it!"

I sat at a metal bench as I waited, she soon came back to the cash register and I paid the bill, she even rolled the cart out to my van and loaded the three bags of groceries.

I of course told her what happened to me and that I was writing a book about it, she said that she was a reader and asked me what the title would be,

"I escaped the grip of the Grim Reaper into a new and beautiful life," she said,

"Wow, that's a long title, but your story sounds interesting!"

She asked when would it be available, I said the book should be out by early autumn, I tried to give her a few dollars for her helping me, she declined saying she wasn't allowed to take tips.

Soon after that I was able to walk from my living room all the way out to my van and back without my walker, this distance was well over a hundred feet so I was getting stronger. I even changed the spark plugs in my van. This was just a week after Marcia left, or less than a month since I was released from the hospital.

I soon decided to have a yard sale, Marcia and I being flea market entrepreneurs, and we owned two fully furnished homes.

We had two or three of everything you can imagine, coffee makers, toasters, microwave ovens and tools. I had a tool box in our home in Pittsburgh fully loaded and one down in North Carolina, I had three power saws, I had three table saws, and I couldn't take everything back home to Pittsburgh, and the way I was feeling about things and about just enjoying my life I just didn't need all of this anymore.

I put an advertisement in the paper for a yard sale. I bit off more than I could chew, I dragged boxes and boxes out to the garage, my legs were killing me, and I had these yard sales for two straight weeks.

This one man looked at my DeWalt saws all, for you that may not know what a 'saws all' may be, since I will mention one again, it's much like a 'jig saw' only bigger and a lot more powerful. I must have paid $100 for it just a year before this and only used it twice.

He asked what I wanted for it, I told him $30, he plugged it in, and it was just fine! He offered $25. I said no, he persisted, I kept firm on $30, but he kept insisting on giving me $25. I then asked,

"Is that all you have?" he answered rudely,

"No, I have lots of money!"

This man just had to beat me down! I finally said,

"Go home!" he just looked at me and I said again, this time a lot more deliberate,

"Go home!"

This man stormed out of my garage got into his car and drove away. I try to be nice but I'm not going to give in to some of these people. It was only a $5 difference!

The price of a 'Big Mac and fries!'

One of these people who came to my yard sales must have seen that I was somewhat disabled and took advantage of me. One night because I didn't pull the garage door down all of the way and that I even left a

I Escaped the Grip of the Grim Reaper

light on throughout the nights, someone came to my home and pulled the door open and stole a lot of my tools. I heard something but it wasn't until six in the morning that I called the police and made a report of it and what was missing.

I turned the loss in through my insurance and in retrospect I probably got more money even with the deductible, for the tools that I would have received from the yard sale.

There was a good thing that happened at my yard sale, I guess you can call it a good thing!

Before I was hospitalized and while I was finishing my book,

"Fire at the flea market,"

Marcia was going through the records that fortunately weren't there at the time of the fire, we were 'pack rats,' we still had close to fifteen hundred 12 inch LP vinyl records at home. This was partly why we thought about waiting another year to move back to Pittsburgh permanently.

There was so much to take back, and then we would sell our home down there. Marcia cleaned probably a thousand records. Country records, the old black artist LPs, and bands like Foghat, Pat Benatar, records that never sold very well for us, but maybe a record store can sell them. She put many in new paper sleeves, and put plastic covers on them. She loaded them into my big Dodge van.

We were going to take them all down to a record store in Charlotte, to hopefully sell them all at once 'cheap,' just to get rid of them. She loaded them side by side covering the whole floor to make it easier for the record store people to view them.

The last time I saw all of these boxes of records she had four boxes of my prized collection of the Beatles, Jimi Hendrix, Pink Floyd and so forth that if the record store would give me a reasonable price on these, I'd sell them too. She placed them at the rear door of the van.

Then this death and coma thing happened to me, I was in the hospital for the next thirty days, and then Marcia would soon leave me.

While I was changing the spark plugs in my van; I opened the back door and saw that most of the records were gone except for a few boxes in the front, behind the seats. I never opened the side door to see what those boxes contained.

I flipped out!

I thought that Marcia took them including my prized collection. When her stepson came down with a big U-Haul truck to get her belongings, I didn't watch what they were taking.

After this happened I couldn't find my prized collection of comic books either, those again fortunately were not at the flea market at the time of the fire.

This collection of well over four hundred super hero comic books from the 1960s, all in great condition and were worth a lot of money. I thought that Marcia took these too, and she didn't bother to call me for ten days or so after she left me.

During this time when I had the yard sale, this one guy saw some of the records I still had in the back room. He asked what I wanted for them, I told him fifty cents each, or cheaper if he bought a lot of them.

Now you have to understand, I was still very much disabled, he then looks through the window of my van and sees the four boxes of records and asked,

"How much do you want for all of them, the ones in the van and in the back room?"

I told him $100 for all of them. He surely liked that price! He starts to load the records from the back room, one box at a time.

I'm thinking damn, I sure have a lot of records even after Marcia took most of them. He must have taken ten boxes to his car.

By the way for those who may still own records, these are boxes I have been getting from the liquor stores for years, 'whisky boxes,' are perfect for records, they are usually just over twelve inches wide and they hold fifty or so records, so they're not too heavy. I would cut holes in these boxes for your finger tips with a utility knife and duct tape them all over for strength, I have used dozens of rolls of duct tape over the years just for my records.

After this man loaded the boxes from the back room he then asked me to open the van but I couldn't find the keys, so I promised him the records when I found them.

He was alright with that, and I gave him my phone number.

After the yard sale for the day and as I was having dinner I found my keys to the van!

Right behind the coffee maker!

I Escaped the Grip of the Grim Reaper

Marcia still hasn't called me yet. I assumed that she took my records and comic books as some kind of collateral for me to keep my promise of giving her all of the money from the sale of our North Carolina home.

The next morning, I started the yard sale again. I was then able to open the van to get at these four boxes of records I promised to give to the guy that bought my records.

To my amazement the boxes still in the van were the four boxes of my prized collection,

"Oh my God,"

I thought, Marcia didn't take them, she just moved them from the back of the van to the front behind the seats. I immediately thought, this guy isn't going to get these records, no way!

He already got more than five hundred great records, all cleaned with new paper record sleeves and plastic covers on each for a mere $100, so I locked up the van again and took the keys in the house just in case this guy came by. Later in the day he called me to ask if I found the keys, I told him,

"No, I guess I'll have to call a locksmith to have a key made."

So I lied, big deal, I hate liars but sometimes it's one of those necessary evils!

This guy called the day after that again, by this time I was getting upset, I told him I found the keys but I was leaving the next day to go back to Pittsburgh, and I had loaded lots of my things on top of the records. He had the nerve to ask,

"Well! Can't you unload your things to get to the records?"

I said,

"Listen, didn't you get enough for your $100?" He then said,

"Yeah, I guess so."

I was still disabled and he knew it, 'what is wrong with people today?' I should write another book about just that subject!

I would later learn by Marcia finally calling me that there were lots of great records like the Beatles and Led Zeppelin even in the records that this guy got, and that she took all of them to the back bedroom except for my prized collection while I was in the hospital. Marcia was so upset that I gave them away for only $100. So he got a great deal.

Period! End of story!

She then told me she had hid my prized comic book collection in the back bedroom closet under a pile of blankets, and get this! She hid them because my loving daughter and her husband were coming down.

"Yeah, Marcia knows my daughter!"

I tell this story because with every bad thing that ever happens to me, there's always a silver lining to it, I do have a habit of misplacing keys, I have so many of them, was it fate that I couldn't find my keys that day?

I surely think so!

Chapter 9: Still no Sheep!

"The sheep were led to slaughter," is a term that implies that people often believe everything they are told, and they don't have a mind of their own, or have you ever heard the term?

"Drinking the Kool-Aid?" deriving from the Guyana mass suicide in which nearly one thousand cult followers were told to drink these paper cups of Kool-Aid containing poison. The cult members knew they would all die, but they drank it anyway! We are,

"A nation of sheep," as told by Judge Andrew Napolitano,

The judge is a Fox news contributor,

He writes about how we as a nation don't always think for ourselves and that we believe everything we hear.

I am not one of these people!

To coin a phrase from a John Mellencamp song,

"I fight authority,"

I have been fighting authority all of my life, and I often win! If I was a 'sheep,' or a 'follower,' I would have metal rods in my neck today!

Please allow me to tell you a little personal story.

This is about who I am!

I had this story in the book about the flea market fire, but since I never published that book and it's a cool story, I thought I'd put it in this book.

Sometime in April 2011, when Marcia and I were still together, we went to a local Walmart in Pittsburgh near where we lived at that time in Roscoe Pa.

Marcia said that we needed a new lawn mower and some groceries. When we arrived there I went into one door where they have the lawn supplies, as Marcia went into the other door for the groceries. I told her I would come back in and meet her at the door after I bought the lawn mower, Marcia said,

"Ok, that's fine!"

I purchased the lawn mower, put it into a shopping cart, and headed out to the parking lot. I opened the tailgate and placed the mower into the back of the van.

I then went back to the store and sat at a bench by the door. I soon met up with Marcia.

We then went to our van, and placed the groceries inside.

As we finished, I noticed that the parking spot in front of us was empty. I figured that I would simply pull straight ahead to exit.

No longer do they put those stupid concrete dividers at parking lots. Once, a long time ago, I dragged the bottom of a car and lost my muffler on one of those damn things.

The parking space next to the space ahead of us was open too, but someone left their cart there after loading their things. I asked Marcia to return it to the cart station just a few feet away.

I started the van and pulled half way up into the empty parking space ahead of me.

Marcia returned; I had to stop momentarily for her to enter the van. Just then a vehicle suddenly pulled in ahead of me, blocking my exit.

This vehicle was some kind of big SUV. This motorist could have easily taken the next space after she saw me trying to pull out, but instead, she just stayed there. She expected that I would back out of my area to allow her to pull all the way in.

But I would not back out. So we were at an impasse or even a good old-fashioned Mexican stand-off.

She wouldn't back out to allow me to pull out ahead and simply be nice about it and park in the very next space, and I would not back up out of my parking space.

This stand-off lasted a good five minutes, I swear!

I stared at the woman, but she would not even look my way; only an occasional glance as she acted as if she was reading something in her lap.

There were no words exchanged between the two of us, no gestures, like the middle finger, nothing. Marcia began to yell at me,

"Just back up, and let's go!"

I demanded,

"No! I was here first. She is being just as stubborn as I."

By this time somebody else parked in the space beside this woman.

Marcia again asked me to not make a big deal about it and just back out. I then insisted,

"She could have easily taken the next space after she saw what I was trying to do."

I felt, why is it me that always has to give in? So I refused to budge.

Then, this woman decided she would just leave her vehicle right where it was and go into the Walmart. She shut her vehicle off, and started to walk towards the store. When I saw this, I realized that I would have to back out after all, but after only a few steps she looked back at her vehicle, and saw that it was just sticking out too far into the parking lane.

She turned around, walked back to her vehicle and without looking my way. She angrily got back in her vehicle, and finally backed out, and parked far away from me! I was then finally able to drive the rest of the way through the space ahead of me and exit.

So I guess I won that battle.

Or did I?

Why was it important for me to win? Marcia then agreed that I was in the right, or was she just appeasing me? Marcia is a completely non-confrontational type of person. In fact, I guess she was a sheep in this saga also, when I think about it now, if it weren't for me making a big fuss over the whole flea market fire thing two years ago, she would also be there selling at the new flea market today.

I feel people are just plain selfish today. In this parking lot episode, did this woman use her vehicle as a type of weapon to exact some kind of personal defiance on me? Or was it I who stood my ground to compensate for my own otherwise inadequate life?

Maybe both are true!

But it was so funny! "I guess you had to be there."

I still tell people about it!

Chapter 10: Going home—to PA!

On March 1st 2012, after wanting to leave each of the last few days, I finally got my nerve up and left to go back to my home in Pittsburgh. My big Dodge van was loaded to the top, I left a lot there but I wasn't ever going back.

I was afraid to go, could my legs take this four-hundred mile trip, and I would have to stop and refuel, and perhaps stop to eat!

At five o'clock in the morning as I was putting the last things in the van when my precious cat Buffy got out of the door, I wasn't about to go out chasing her in the dark so regretfully I just left her down there. I'm so sorry!

There were a few stay cats in the area so I dumped the last of her bag of cat food on the back deck and soon left, I do miss her!

The trip went well though; I kept thinking how happy I was that I would never have to go to my North Carolina home again.

I put the home up for sale with Genesis Realty from Kannapolis, NC, a week before I left.

This is where the famous NASCAR driver Dale Earnhardt Senior was from. He died in a rather harmless looking crash at the Daytona 500 in 2001. Now, NASCAR requires that all drivers use this thing called the Hans neck brace.

I arrived at my home in Roscoe, Pa. at a little after three o'clock in the afternoon. I then called my real estate friend Tom to meet me because I always gave him my keys when I left for the winters. He helped me unload most of my things, and there I was home at last. The next day I picked up my friend Stanley and he helped me unpack the rest of my things.

Chapter 11: Giving back!

In late March, I thought I'd go to a flea market in Perryopolis, not far from my home in Roscoe, Pa. It was a Sunday, and it was calling for rain. It was also pretty cold that morning, taking my walker and just $100 with me. On the way I changed my mind, I figured; why not go to the flea market where Frank may be working for the day?

Frank is an old friend of mine and I'd like to see him again. This flea market, once a brand new Lowe's movie theater, failed after two short years so now it's an inside and outside flea market. The nearly forty mile drive to North Versailles, Pa. would take an hour to get there but I went anyway!

I arrived at seven o'clock in the morning, parked my red Dodge Caravan and headed out to the area where the outside vendors set up.

I decided not to use my walker!

There was Frank, sitting in his dark green mini-van. I was pleased. As I neared his van he shouted out,

"Bad Bob!" I then yelled back,

"Bad Frank!"

That's how we always greeted each other!

He wasn't set up yet,

"Come and sit in my van," Frank said.

As I was sitting there he said,

"Bob, you lost some weight!"

I then replied,

"Frank, it's easy to lose weight when you're in a coma!" Frank then asked,

"What do you mean you were in a coma? What happened?"

I told him the whole story, about how joining the YMCA led to my dying, the coma, the delusions I had and so forth, I told him how happy I was now that this happened to me, and how I was writing a book about the whole experience. He then said,

"Bob, I've known you for over twenty years, and I've said this before," then he laughed,

"You can fall in shit and come out smelling like a rose!" I then said,

"Frank, you're right, it seems like in all of my life, when bad things happened, some- thing good always came from it."

Yes, he was right, maybe because I have determination, and maybe God looks over me. There's a saying, I'm not quite how it goes, but God looks over the dumb and stupid, and I've surely been both.

We both laughed and talked about the good old days for an hour or so about the antique deal we once made; the Avon buy we once were involved in, and a Bronze statue that I will soon write about. I asked,

"Why are you setting up so early in the season? It's only March and it's too cold yet!" He said,

"Bob, if I don't pay the light company $60 by Tuesday they're shutting my power off!"

I immediately pulled my wallet out of my back pocket, pulled out $60 and tried to hand it to him. He said,

"Bob, I don't want your money," I said,

"Frank, it's a gift, this is the new me, what good is money if you can't help an old friend?"

We argued back and forth until he accepted the money and thanked me,

"Bob, I didn't even have the money to set up, I was hoping to be able to talk the guy into waiting for the $15 set up fee," I then asked,

"Do you want more?"

"No, no, please," Frank replied.

"Do you want a coffee?" I asked,

"Yes, just cream," He tried to hand me one of the $20's, I just walked off. When I got back from getting the coffees, I asked Frank to run the engine for heat, He said,

"Ok, but for just a minute my oil light is on!"

"Well put some oil in!" I calmly demanded.

"I have a bad oil pan gasket, I tried putting some silicone around the lip but it didn't work." Frank then said.

Here we go again, I said, "Frank, let me buy you another vehicle, not a new one but just a little mini-van for say $1,500 or so."

"Come on Bob, I'm not going to let you do that besides it has a good motor and transmission," Frank answered.

I Escaped the Grip of the Grim Reaper

"Well ok, but let me pay to have this one fixed," I demanded!

We argued for a while until he agreed, but it would cost $140, and since I didn't have that much on me at the time, we agreed that he would take it to the garage the next day, and he would call me and have me give my credit card numbers to the manager so he could debit the amount from my checking account.

He wrote my phone number down on a piece of paper, I even went to the Walmart next to the flea market and bought him a five quart bottle of oil, for him to have oil in the engine until he had the oil pan gasket replaced.

Well folks, he never did call me, he's just too proud. I will see him soon, maybe one day I'll just buy everything on his tables whether I can use the items or not, ha, ha.

This is the way I feel now, sure, I still have to watch my money but I have enough to help someone, not just anyone. I would never help a drug addict or a drunk, and I have plenty childhood friends that went that way, they chose to live that kind of life.

Frank is a black man, I haven't mentioned that. I guess I just see him as a man, a good man! With him I just don't see color.

This man and I have had quite a few fascinating adventures since I met him way back in 1992 at a flea market in North Versailles Pa. I've eaten at his home, the first time he poured me a cup of coffee, I wasn't watching him, when I drank it I cried out,

"Frank, this is horrible! It has coffee grounds in it!"

Frank laughed,

"It's what we old timers call hobo coffee Bob!"

I uttered,

"Ok," and continued sipping the coffee. Soon after we got to know each other at the flea market he came over to my booth,

"Bob, let me show you something," he pulled a tattered photograph from his wallet, it was some kind of five foot tall bronze statue with serpent heads sticking out from their necks in different directions.

"This is a statue from the Sung Dynasty of China!"

He proceeded to tell me the story of how he was called by some old woman from Homewood Pa, a small town just out of the city of Pittsburgh, Homewood just like Braddock, was once a bustling town, it's now just another ghetto full of drugs and drive by shootings. Frank goes on with this story of how he was hired to clean out this woman's basement.

As he fills his truck with stuff that he would sell at the flea market the next weekend, he eventually spots this statue in a corner of the basement with spider webs all over it, he calls upstairs for the woman to come down and asks if she wants him to take that away too, the woman says,

"Yes Frank, throw that away too,"

Frank is an honest man, he told her that he may get a lot of money for it and tells her,

"Ma'am, I'm not charging you to clean out your basement, I actually want to give you $50,"

She was delighted and accepted the money. He told me he later sold this statue for $2,700 and today it's at a museum somewhere in New York City.

Another time at the flea market he says to me that he had a chance to buy a house full of antique furniture for $1,000 but he only had half of the money and asked if I would like to go in on it with him, I said,

"Sure Frank, I have the money,"

"We'll split the money we make," Frank then said.

I met him at a gas station the very next morning in that same town of Homewood. He was waiting in his old red pickup truck with three other black men, one sitting with him up front and two sitting in the back of the truck. One white man may think,

"What did I just get myself into?"

I shut off my vehicle and locked it of course and went to Frank, and gave him my share of the deal, he said,

"Thank you Bob, jump in the back of the truck!"

So here I am sitting in the back of a truck with these two young black men, not a word was spoken!

Thank God the trip to this house was just a couple of blocks. When we got to this home an old man was waiting, Frank had told me that this man's wife had died and that he was moving in with family. Frank handed this man the $1,000 and all of us went into the home.

We went upstairs to the bedrooms, Frank told the men to gently remove all of the drawers and take the furniture downstairs further stating to arrange the rooms into a circle separated suit by suit.

I went to pull a drawer out and Frank yelled,

"Bob, let these fellows do it!"

I didn't even have to do any of the work. Frank is also a very smart man, he already had buyers scheduled to come to this house!

After all of the furniture was downstairs Frank gave these three young men $25 each and sent them away. Within the next hour he sold two bedroom sets for $3,000.

He then sold the living room and dining room sets to another man for $3,000 and a beautiful huge round oak kitchen table and two chairs for an additional $1,000.

We also took four or five boxes full of small antiques such as clocks, old radios and some old jewelry out to the truck, in which we sold over the next few months for well over $500 more and split that too.

Frank and I later would go to a little restaurant on the south side of Pittsburgh for cheese burgers and fries with Frank saying,

"Today, we live like Kings!"

Frank also once cut me in on a deal for Avon products which earned me nearly $2,000. Those were the good old days.

I went to work at the old inside flea market that has since been torn down one Saturday back in October 1995. I was all happy with a big smile on my face and showing off a pile of old $100 bills, Frank asks,

"What do you have there?"

"Frank this is just a small sample of what I found in my kitchen cabinets," I replied.

I proceeded to tell him my story of how I found $19,000 in the Lazy Susan of the house I bought the prior year, and that he helped me move into. I was looking for the power cord to my Camcorder because I was having my roof replaced at that time and needed all the money I could muster. I was so broke that I had only $1.32 left in my checking account, and I was going to sell the Camcorder at the flea market the coming weekend.

I told him that I thought that the cord might have fallen through the space between the turnstile and the cabinet, so I squeezed my hand into the space and with my fingers felt what seemed to be a plastic envelope, I pulled this old Mellon bank envelope out still on my knees. I opened the envelope,

I was astonished to see that it was filled with $100 bills. I got up from the floor and put these bills in piles of $1,000 on my kitchen table.

I had fourteen of these piles, I again put my hand into that space of the Lazy Susan cabinet and struggling with my finger-tips, felt a small metal box, and slowly pulled it out of the cabinet, it was an old Band-aid box, and I counted $5,000 more in $100 bills and a few $20 bills.

I then went to the basement and brought my Craftsman reciprocating 'saws all' upstairs and cut the metal turnstile out of the cabinet only to find nothing else, I was just a little upset, I ruined a perfectly good Lazy Susan cabinet.

One might say that I had an obligation because of some law that I had heard of to give this money to the previous owner who died some years earlier, or to his family, but this old house that I ironically paid $19,000 for stood empty for six years and a lot of the windows were broken, and from what I heard by talking to the old owners nephew, is that this man also once owned the bar across the street, and that the new owner after he purchased the bar found nearly $50,000 in the basement!

I guess this man perhaps hid some of his money from the IRS.

Thank you old man!

The morning that I found this money the three man crew came to finish my roof, this crew, old friends from Braddock, worked cheap. Dale the boss; is the best roofer there is, he only charged me $1,000 for the job, with me paying almost that amount for the materials.

I helped them in picking up the old broken slate, put them in plastic garbage cans, and took the cans up the road to a man that was looking for a 'clean fill'. I also carried bundles of shingles up the ladders and set them on the edge of the roof.

When I buy homes I always buy one with a good roof, I can climb a ladder with no problem but when it comes to making that first step onto the actual roof, I freeze up in fear, I just can't do it!

I paid Dale the $1,000 that day and then gave him and the two other men $100 extra. While they were finishing up; I drove to a gas station and bought them each a carton of 'Marlboros'.

I even took the three of them to lunch at a local Italian restaurant, spent $70 and gave the waitress a $20 tip!

What a day that was!

I Escaped the Grip of the Grim Reaper

And in hindsight there was no way that this fat cord with some type of voltage regulator attached to it, could have just fallen into this little gap, by the way I never did find the cord!

Just a little more of my falling into shit and coming out smelling like a rose!

Today, things aren't going too well for Frank; he used to rent his own antique store but had to give it up, now he sets up at the flea market with just a few things each weekend just trying to get by. The way I figure it 'I owed him!' so it was a pleasure to give back to this proud black man.

I have a friend named Stanley, I mentioned him earlier; this man and I grew up five houses from each other in Braddock, and we are still friends today. Stanley is Polish and he speaks broken English, kids picked on him in school, I even picked on him, everybody called him Stush.

Years later he asked me to start calling him Stanley! I complied with his wishes, so I guess he grew up feeling inferior in some way. He tried to join the Navy with me on a buddy system but failed the tests, years later he told me he failed the tests on purpose because he really didn't want to join.

Through no fault of his own making, He never really had a job. He worked at a Starbucks for a short time and then through a club-house program that he joined more or less to get out of the house and meet people acquired a job working in a county office building doing minimal jobs as some type of messenger.

He has gone to school for electronics and then electric tech school but still he's never accomplished much of anything, I would sometimes hire him to help me with my houses, and to be honest I never paid him much, I took advantage of him. Now he's on SSI disability for so-called mental problems, he told a doctor that he was,

"Hearing voices!"

One day I called him when I was at my North Carolina home recovering from my death experience. I asked him if he was ever going to get his drivers permit. He said that his sister doesn't have time to take him out for driving lessons. I interrupted him by saying that I would pay for his own driver training, he said no of course, it would cost up to $400.

I said,

"So what, I'll pay for it!"

He asked why I would do that, I explained the same way I did with Frank, he agreed to that but when I offered to buy him a used car for up to $3,000 he refused the offer, after a while of arguing he accepted my offer but changed his mind when we talked again the next day.

As mentioned, the day after I came back home to Pittsburgh I had him help me for the day unpacking the rest of my van and another old van full of flea market stuff, he also helped me set up my computer. I handed him a wad of money laughing,

"Here's $300 and I'm not giving you another nickel!"

Just a way of my, 'giving back!'

Chapter 12: Fate!

I've always believed in fate, and it surely applies here. When the flea market burned down in September of 2010, as mentioned I wrote a book about the fire. I finished the book but never had it published,

I will soon be finishing the book and also write a thriller I wrote some fifteen years ago. Yes, I am a writer at heart, at least I think I can be one, If I can only apply myself and not be in such a hurry, I've had so much trouble in writing this book and I'm so scared that it still isn't right,

"Gosh, I never even finished high school!"

Please be gentle with me with your criticism after all as stated in my preface this book is written,

"In my own words!"

I may not know a lot of long fancy words, but I do know a few, and maybe my grammar is a little suspect but I am from Braddock, (you know!) I am a 'things to do today,' sort of man. I write down my chores for the day and I've been doing this for as long as I can remember. I think I need to express my thoughts on paper, but when you work for a living it's hard to stick with it! Writing is so very hard!

It's truly a 'CRAFT'! The word craft will always stick in my mind, thank you Cynthia! (My little secret)

Today it is so much easier with this thing right here, a personal computer and the tools available.

So what about fate? After the initial drama of the fire and having to sell our home and move back to Pittsburgh, and this thing happening to me, is it fate? That now I'm writing a book, a 'good book' I hope!

Although I feel so different now, I feel enlightened, I feel smarter, I feel more relaxed but I still take no shit from anyone.

Here I am, writing a book about how this thing that happened to me, and all I write about is bad things, the guy with my records, the man and the 'saw's all' drama, Marcia leaving me, the Walmart stand-off and of course Chapter 5, My loving daughter,

I can also write about a notorious huge price gouging plumbing and electrical company in the Pittsburgh area by the name of Gillece, in which I had to go to court over my sewer backing up during the Easter weekend, but I won't!

All I will say is just look up pissedconsumer.com, type Gillece in on the search bar and read,

"Gillece and its' terrorist threats against me and my property."

You will find my story!

And I can write a bad story about Time Warner, a cable company that most of us have heard of.

Perhaps, I will someday soon in another book!

This book is supposed to be about my death, my coma, and my new and beautiful life!

I never meant this to be an autobiography, but I guess it is!

Imagine that! An unknown common ordinary man writing about himself!

How dare I?

When I wrote early in the book about my times in the US Navy I didn't mention everything. When I first joined the Navy I was told by my recruiter that I would join my brother Stephen, not mentioned until now, on this 'Brother,' program that the Navy had, and I would be stationed at the Patuxent River naval air base.

I was lied to by the recruiter and sent to this ship after boot camp instead!

I was just a young stupid kid;

I was not the America loving person I am today.

"I was a non-conformist!"

I started to smoke marijuana, and Hashish, I took pills and even LSD a few times.

But honestly I wasn't that bad!

One time as I was sitting in the mess hall with friends and I was speaking the old 'hippie' jargon, by saying, "Yeah man! And Right On!"

Some petty officer walked by and thought I was high on drugs and he led me to the medical clinic for a urine test. The test for drugs was negative but they still ordered me to go 'not to drug rehab' but to drug awareness classes.

After I graduated so to speak, and then after I got into a fist fight with a fellow shipmate and broke his jaw the chief petty officer of my department demanded that I sign papers making me responsible for his hospital bills.

I refused to sign the papers!

He then simply asked,

"Robert, do you want out of the Navy?"

Of course I answered,

"Yes I do!"

Needless to say, I received an Honorable Discharge after serving three years of a four year enlistment but with hidden 'unable to adapt to military life' intangibles.

I remember my Executive Officer calling me over the PA broadcasting system to go to his office chambers and saying,

"Robert, I understand that you quit high school to join the Navy, and now you're quitting the Navy. Are you setting a pattern for the rest of your life?"

I still remember those words!

I am a man of determination, and I am no quitter!

And perhaps that is why I came back from the dead!

"I had unfinished business!"

Today, my life is still hard and maybe I'm just fooling myself. The world is a bad place, and has many bad and evil people in it. While I claim to have changed and to be so different, the rest of the world didn't change when I died on December 17, 2011.

People are even worse today, we all are so consumed with our own little world earning a living, paying ever increasing gas prices, feeding our family that we have lost our compassion for each other!

What happened at a movie theater in Aurora, Colorado and at a Sikh temple in Wisconsin are just examples of the pure hate people have for each other these days!

Then the un-thinkable happens in Newtown, Connecticut, with the murdering of all of those beautiful children!

I really believe that we are in the 'Ends of Time!'

How do you keep a smile on your face and live a truly great life when we don't even know, nor want to know our neighbors?

I will still maintain my new attitude of living my life as complete as possible.

Chapter 13: Present day!

I joined the local YMCA up here in the Pittsburgh area near the end of March of 2012,

"Not so much sugar this time!"

It's an old facility in Monongahela, Pa. This Y is not nearly as nice as the YMCA down in Salisbury, NC, but it's just fine.

This one even has an outdoor pool! I spend most of the time in the hot tub, trying to get my legs from hurting so much and I'm still getting my strength and endurance back.

While I was in the indoor pool one day I was telling Amy, a young and pretty life-guard about what happened to me and that I was writing a book about it, she grabbed her towel and sat at the edge of the pool right next to me.

"Go on, tell me more!" This is the reaction I get when I tell my story, gosh! I probably have a thousand books sold already!"

I continued to tell her all about what my loving daughter did to me, and that I wrote a special chapter just for her. I also told her of the happiness I feel today because of what happened!

On April 13, 2012 I had the deep wrinkles or frown lines on my forehead taken care of. Just a few Botox injections took care of that.

This was just a temporary fix; I was told that I would need to have it done again in six months, and to perhaps have a Dermabrasion done also.

My Zodiac sign is Aquarius, not that I read my horoscope every day, but I read once that some Aquarians tend to have an odd look about them, not ugly, just a little peculiar like Abraham Lincoln or Duane Chapman of 'Dog, bounty hunter.'

I've been told that I look like a character on a popular show called 'Deadliest catch' I never really watched this program, but it's about crab fishing.

This young girl once came up to me a few years ago at Idle Wild, an amusement park near Latrobe Pa, saying,

"You look just like that guy on the Deadliest catch!"

I just recently looked up the show on the internet and saw this guy, he does look like me but not so much now that I lost weight, but he's not a bad looking man, so I don't mind the reference.

I recently joined the Slovak club again here in Roscoe, Pa. I was a member since 2008 but I never went much, I joined to meet new people in the new area but it seemed to me that there was some kind of 'Clique' there and I wasn't a part of it!

Besides that, I don't think that sitting in a bar all night is that much fun even though if you were to read my hospital release papers they say that I suffer with 'Alcoholism.'

'What a Joke!'

The day before I had my Botox procedure done I lost a good friend!

I'll call him Sonny;

I've known Sonny for the past twelve years, he was once the karaoke DJ at the bar where I met Marcia, and we became good friends. We talked on the phone all of time while I stayed in North Carolina and was real sympathetic when this death and coma thing happened to me.

While I was driving home from shopping at a local Walmart Sonny calls. I told him I was having this Botox procedure done, he immediately yells out,

"Bobby Lee!" he has a big mouth!

"I know this girl, she had the same kind of thing done, and they messed her up man!"

He went on!

"She had a different surgeon try to fix the damage but she won't even leave the house anymore!"

Imagine that! He just happens to know someone who had the same thing done as I was having done! He went on; I tried to interrupt him by saying that having Botox is very safe and that he was exaggerating, and even lying.

I said in a humorous way,

"Sonny, I love you man but you exaggerate too much and you're a habitual liar, but I accept you just the way you are!"

He started yelling,

"What do you mean I'm a habitual liar?"

I Escaped the Grip of the Grim Reaper

Just then I lost the cell phone signal down on this river road on my way home.

I called him back in just a few minutes when I got home and was in my drive way,

He already had put a block on my phone number! I guess he thought that I hung up on him and was mad at me. Damn, I was only telling him the truth but I told him that I loved him, how could he be so sensitive?

But it was alright for him to yell out that I was ugly twice over the years when he called out my name to sing at his Karaoke gigs.

The next day I left my phone in the car while I was having the Botox to my forehead done. After the procedure I then went and had a haircut, never looking at my phone yet.

I then went to visit Bobby, Marcia's son and his wife Janet, seeing them for the first time since I was back from North Carolina.

As I sat on their couch showing off my new forehead, the Botox was already working. I looked at my cell phone, there were eight voice messages and they were all from Sonny.

Each of these messages ran out of time and I don't have any type of special time limit on my messaging!

He called again and again, first telling me how mad he was at me and that he never wanted to talk to me again, then he changed his attitude saying how he valued my friendship and then he went back to hating me saying that I changed after my death experience for the worse.

He was wrong! I just got smarter, now I see him as a man who needs to make up these stories to make him-self seem more interesting.

He also said that he never wanted me to come to his Karaoke gigs again; then he called again, leaving another message that he never wanted to talk to me again and that I needed to see a psychiatrist.

I thought it was he who needed to see a psychiatrist! For someone who never wanted to talk to me again, then why is he calling me over and over again, leaving these messages.

The few days after that, while I was putting my swimming trunks on at the YMCA, he called, I did answer this time! He yells out,

"Bobby Lee, I just want you to know that my phone was messed up, Verizon put a block on the whole 724 grid on my phone!" 724 coincidentally is my area code,

"Imagine that!"

I get into a small argument with him, I lose signal, I call him back five minutes later and my number is blocked but not only is my number blocked, every phone in the Pittsburgh area is blocked with the area code 724. I say again,

"Imagine that!"

I immediately say,

"There you go, starting another conversation with a lie," and I hung up!

Before I could write this story, I thought I should call my own cell phone provider AT&T to ask if this whole area code blocking by your cell phone provider was possible.

I talked to a Carlos Gallagher, atwenty-nine year old man from technical support, after telling him I needed this information for my book, he told me that what Sonny said was highly un-likely!

We talked about what happened to me and the book I was writing, he asked that I put his name in the book, he then added,

"I haven't had a conversation this interesting in all of the eighteen years that I've been here."

Thanks Carlos!

This Sonny is an exaggerator and yes, he is a habitual liar.

I won't go to the bar to sing anymore if that's the way he wants it!

Before we had this altercation he called me while I was working in one of my rentals,

"Bobby Lee, I'm so pissed off!" I asked why of course, he went on without taking a breath, about how his girlfriend was DJ-ing at a bar in Duquesne, Pa.

One of the patrons put an ice pick to one of his tires on his brand new 2012 KIA SUV. She called him to come to this bar but when he got there he couldn't find the spare tire. He had to have the KIA towed and it cost him $470 for the tow and storage for the night.

He went on and on to tell me that the dealership told him that the spare tire or the jack wasn't even manufactured yet and wasn't going to be available until sometime in the summer, he continued with his gibberish again without taking a breath or allowing me to say a word.

This is a guy that you can hold your phone away from your ear for five or even ten minutes pull it back to your ear and he's still talking,

I Escaped the Grip of the Grim Reaper

"I've done just that!"

He goes on how he threatened the dealership that he wasn't going to make any more payments until this problem of not having a spare tire or the jack to change the tire was solved.

I actually believed his story at first, but since we got into this huge argument over the Botox thing I thought I'd investigate this story.

I called three different KIA dealerships in the area, and they all told me that this is a lie and that every new vehicle has a spare tire and a jack, and that it was against the law not to provide these.

Sonny is a pot smoker, not just a pot smoker. He's been smoking too much pot for too many years, he's high all of the time, over the years he has told me some wild and unbelievable stories.

I still consider him to be my friend, but he needs to grow up and stop smoking so much pot. I guess I finally had enough when he told me of the girl and her Botox story.

I know this was a long story about Sonny but he was a big part of my life for all of these years, and I will miss going to his gigs. He is the best at his profession! He spares no expenses on the newest technology in his Karaoke equipment.

He no longer carries thousands of discs everywhere he goes, he has it all in a computer and with his adjusting of the system he can make the worst singers sound pretty good.

So Sonny, if you read this book, I still love you man! I'm sorry that we aren't friends anymore.

Back in January 2010, while I was at my so-called winter home in North Carolina helping Marcia with the flea market duties I had to come back to Pittsburgh just to evict a tenant who thought after not paying her rent and not answering her phone that I wouldn't dare come back in the dead of winter to evict her.

I sure fooled her!

But then I was stuck here when a blizzard hit and produced thirty inches of snow, I lost power as well as a few thousand other people for three days.

Since I lost power I wound up re-joining the Slovak club for $20 just to watch the Indianapolis Colts lose to the New Orleans Saints in Super Bowl XLIV, and I never went back until now.

Since I was now back home this past April I decided to work on my little apartment, I bought this home in Roscoe in 2008, it was much too big to have just a single family living in it, so I made it into a three bedroom apartment to rent and a small one bedroom apartment for myself, the two car garage is attached to my side, so I alone use it.

The kitchen needed work, I put in a new window in, scrubbed the beautiful cabinets, painted, put up a lot of shelves up to sort all of my things, I am a shelf builder, I have probably put up three hundred shelves in my time in all of the homes I have lived in or renting them and I'm not exaggerating!

I also put in blue carpet squares in, nothing special, just for myself.

I then put an advertisement in the local newspaper and put two signs in the windows to find a new tenant for the three bedroom apartment connected to my little place.

This young lady Nancy called. When she said that she had four children, I was skeptical. Four kids, running up and down the stairs right next to me!

I still agreed to show her the apartment. She brought her kids, all girls, ages from fifteen to her infant of one year.

I liked her girls right away, and I figured that I wouldn't be living in the little apartment very long anyway for I really wanted to eventually live in North Versailles Pa, a town where I lived previously, and close to all of my friends including Marcia's son Bobby.

Nancy told me when she called the advertisement, the phone number was disconnected, but luckily she drove around the town and saw my number on the 'for rent,' signs in the windows!

This is just a little more of the incompetence that I feel is going on with our county these days,

When I called to put the Ad in the paper I gave the lady my cell phone number, but she still used my land line phone number that was in their computer records from a previous Ad I put in the newspaper for a different rental and more than a year before this.

Nancy is thirty one years old and, "Hot," real good looking! I would have loved connecting with her but what would she want with an ugly old man like me?

I Escaped the Grip of the Grim Reaper

We became good friends though, and the kids running up and down the steps never bothered me! I told her it was fate that she was now my new tenant; she is also pretty good with a computer and she read a lot of my book.

Nancy had issues though, she had filed for divorce from her husband because of his drinking at social clubs with his 'buddies' all of the time, and he was not at all happy about her leaving.

He sort of harassed her a bit by driving around the house late in the night to see if she was alone.

'You know what I mean!'

Nancy soon quit her job thinking that her husband would pay child support and give her money for the rent.

I even said to her,

"Nancy, why would you quit your job? You're not divorced, and alimony and child support hasn't been determined yet!"

When the rent became due in June, she didn't have it, I just paid a huge amount of money to that Gillece plumbing company that I briefly talked about already and I was also evicting another tenant at a different house at the time and I really needed her rent.

She asked if her mother could move in with her to help pay the rent. When you're a land-lord sometimes you're often a social worker too. I would have agreed but her mother had a dog, one of those small barking type of dogs.

The previous tenants that lived there brought a barking dog to the house, at first I didn't care but after a few times when there wouldn't be anyone home they would put this dog in the basement and it would not stop barking, the sound was excruciating as it was intensified by being in an empty basement, I demanded that they get rid of the dog or else I would evict them.

I told Nancy that her mother could move in but not the dog, I knew that wouldn't go over well, so one day when I came home from a long day selling at the flea market Nancy and her kids were gone, she moved back in with her husband.

So, that was that, I wasn't too upset about it, land-lords put up with so much. I just hope that eventually I will be done with this whole business! I still talk to Nancy on the phone and I miss her kids!

Recently again, I went back to the flea market hoping to see my friend Frank again to ask him why he didn't let me pay to have his car fixed.

I was going to set up myself. I loaded my red Caravan up with a lot of records, and comic books. I also loaded a lot of items that came with the house that I bought last year in 2011.

Frank wasn't there, too bad but I'm sure I'll see him soon;

I will sell at the flea markets all spring and summer this year. I also set up at another flea market in Perryopolis, Pa. that following Sunday, and for the first I time I had fun doing this, the weather was nice, not cold and not too hot.

I talked and joked with people, I told my customers of me dying and coming back to life, and the whole story. I wound up having a good weekend making over $400.

April 17, 2012 soon came; I have to mention this date because it would have been the 55th birthday of my brother John. He had a heart attack and died on July 9, 1990. He was only thirty-three years old!

He was a real character, I still miss him, I hope to see him some-day when I die again. He was my right hand man; he helped me a lot with my roofing needs. He did like to drink though! Yeah, I guess he was an alcoholic.

The day he died he was working on an old truck with 'David Aches' doing body work,

David, a friend to John and also to me, was there with him when John suddenly turned blue, he slumped over and died. An ambulance came soon but it was too late. David called me to give me the grim news. We still talk of John; he was surely one of a kind.

These days I'm watching my weight, I do not want to get fat again. I've learned that yogurt tastes just as good as ice cream, and I love sugar free Jell-O. I also munch on baby carrots instead of potato chips, and now instead of soft drinks I drink ice water, a lot of ice water.

While I lost my weight the easiest way possible,

"No hunger pains when you're in a coma!"

Most people fail or regain the weight because they first have to learn to eat the right foods.

Starving yourself just doesn't work!

My weight is holding at two hundred pounds, still a little more than I wish, but by stamina isn't quite right yet, I get tired real fast.

I Escaped the Grip of the Grim Reaper

Well, I finally had a cup of coffee at Starbucks on April 20, 2012. I didn't plan it this way but I went with my real estate agent and friend Tom.

I talked to him one morning, I told him that I needed to go to Lowes to return the old battery from my rider mower and a tool that I didn't need.

I also had to go to PNC bank to deposit a couple of rent payments into a new account since my loving daughter put a freeze on my old account! Tom mentioned that he was going to the same bank.

I asked if he wanted to go to Starbucks for coffee.

I expected him to tell me that he wasn't about to pay $5 for a simple cup of coffee, just like myself.

You see, this man is rich, he owns twenty- seven homes. He also has money invested in some kind of pheasant farm in the Dakotas, but he is the cheapest man I know.

He said he's been to a Starbucks quite a few times. I figured that he probably went on business and that he able to write the cost off on his taxes,

"I just know him so well!"

I offered to buy; and of course he accepted my offer.

I walked into the Starbucks as Tom was in his truck talking on his cell phone; I stood there in the middle of the coffee shop, took a deep breath and uttered,

"Starbucks, at last!"

We then sat outside and enjoyed our coffee, both of us having the Mocha.

Over the last few years Tom and I have helped each other on our rental houses, he would help me when I needed to drag a carpet up a pair of stairs and I would help him to do plumbing sometimes.

On one of these plumbing jobs at one of his rentals we had to go to Lowes building center, I showed him a CPVC one half inch plumbing tee, and said we might need one.

Tom said,

"I think I have one of them at home!"

This plumbing Tee fitting costs twenty cents. He actually wanted to drive a good ten miles in a completely different direction in his gas guzzling truck to find the Tee.

If you as old as I am you might remember a television commercial where a man and a woman are sitting at an outside table, at this beautiful home drinking wine,

The woman asks Mario (I really don't remember the name used,)

"Why would a man of your considerable wealth buy such a reasonably priced wine?"

The man replies,

"How do you think I became a man of considerable wealth?"

Speaking of old commercials and this one has nothing to do with my book but I just thought of it,

"Pardon me sir' but do you have any Grey Poupon?"

"Does that strike your memory?" Grey Poupon is a brand of mustard.

I used to pull up to a car at a red light, open my window and I'd say those words to the other driver, just for kicks, the other driver would laugh or just ignore me! I haven't done this for a long, long time.

Perhaps I'll do this again someday!

I will be going to Kennywood soon also, a popular amusement park not far from Braddock, going there again wasn't on my

"Bucket list!"

But I haven't been there for probably four years, and enjoying my-self was on my bucket list!

I heard they built a new ride called the "Black Widow," I just have to ride it! This park is right across the Monongahela River from Braddock.

As a young teenager, I along with my friends would walk the length of Braddock Avenue, walk across the Rankin Bridge, make a left turn and walk another mile or so to the park just to go swimming at the huge beautiful pool at Kennywood, we did this many times!

Sometimes if and when we all had enough money to pitch in we would stop at Islay's, a famed store and restaurant at 734 Braddock Avenue for a pound of 'chipped ham,' and a loaf of bread.

You can see an old photo of this burned out Islay's store on 'Flickr' on the internet.

We would then sit somewhere and make ourselves sandwiches for the long three mile walk, or else we would stop at the Blue Bird Café, a block away for a tasty hamburger, or else we would stop and buy three hot dogs with their secret family garnishing recipe for a dollar at the Coney Island restaurant, where I was once found sleep-walking!

When I went to the Kennywood pool with just my friend David Aches we would take two different buses and get a ride home from his brother Burgess in his pearl white 1969 Dodge Charger with red leather interior.

"Boy, was that a nice car?"

The pool has since been plowed over and now the area is called the Lost Kenny wood.

In those days my step-father didn't own or want to own a car, he was a 'bookie.' One might say that he was somewhat associated with the mob. He would rather walk or take a bus everywhere.

I remember him well!

His name was Vincent De Paul, there are used clothing thrift shops with that name, I don't think there's any type of connection, and I just always thought it to be a little odd. I remember him being a big man with big thick eye glasses.

I recall my mother telling me that he was once a star football player in high school and was a prospect for a college scholarship but he chose to work at the local Homestead steel mill instead. He hung around his brother Jake a lot for which my mother hated and he wasn't much of a family or a handy man,

I remember my mother yelling at him one time calling him a 'queer,' needless to say they divorced after a few short years.

The thing I remember most of all about the man is that he would put ketchup on everything he ate! I just about died laughing when I once saw him putting ketchup on his mashed potatoes!

When Marcia and I lived in North Carolina we would go food shopping at Food Lion or Walmart and buy chipped ham, they didn't sell Islay's but what they had was Smithfields' brand of ham, it was pretty good but not as good as Islay's, and the counter person would always correct me by asking,

"Do you mean you want it s-h-a-v-e-d?"

I would laugh and say,

"Yes honey, we call it chipped ham in Pittsburgh but please just go ahead and s-h-a-v-e it!"

It was so funny because they would drag the word s-h-a-v-e in their southern accent!

This one time at the lunch meat counter at a Walmart I was just kidding when I asked if they carried Islay's, the man said,

"Yes, we now have Islay's ham!"

I was so happy! I was able to buy my favorite chipped ham, until sometime later I was told that they no longer sold it.

I asked,

"Why not?"

He went on to tell me that the Smithfield ham company demanded that they stop selling Islay's.

I guess they didn't like the competition!

You see that! There are politics even in the chipped ham industry!

Isn't America supposed to be the land of free choice?

"Not when it comes to some lousy chipped ham, I guess! And that's enough of that!"

My real estate friend Tom also owns a cottage in Punxsutawney Pa, the home of Phil the infamous 'Ground-hog.' He has told me in the past that if I ever wanted to go there for a weekend just ask him for the keys. I think I'll take him up on his offer soon. There are a lot of things I want to do, especially this summer.

I still have to work though; my new life isn't just all about having fun. I have that other house in Donora Pa. A cute little 'and I do mean little' one bedroom house that I bought just this past year.

I got it real cheap, and it has a newer roof.

I closed in the front porch and tore out the original front wall to make the living room bigger. You couldn't even put a couch in this living room it was so small. I have done some work to this house but it needs a lot more, perhaps that will be fun!

I do like to work and the exercise will do me good, but I do need to slow down, every day that I work my legs get real sore. The getting down on the floor and then getting back to my feet really kills me!

I'm in no real hurry to finish the house, so I'll take a break from it for a little while.

This coming winter when it's cold, I don't much like going out-doors during the Pittsburgh winters. I think I'll build some models.

When I was a kid I built a bunch of mostly monster models, Frankenstein, the Mummy, Dracula, the Werewolf, and the Hunchback from Notre Dame.

I Escaped the Grip of the Grim Reaper

I had this one model of the Man from U.N.C.L.E, a 1964 television series starring Robert Vaughn as Napoleon Solo, and David McCallum as Lllya Kuryakin.

This model consisted of two different models with one of these characters perched on a brick wall; you would then glue these two models together to make one, I also had a model of the Santa Maria, one of the three ships that Christopher Columbus sailed on to discover America. I hand painted all of my models in great detail.

My mother put up a nice long shelf in my bedroom for my models, I still remember my models!

One day when I was sixteen or so, I wasn't home, my brother Steve and his friend George took my models down to the river and shot them up with a BB gun. The things kids did for kicks back then, but kids today shoot real guns at each other, I might add, just for kicks!

George is also my friend; we lost contact for some twenty years until I saw his sister at a pizza shop, I asked her for his phone number.

At this same time Marcia and I were invited to spend two days and two nights at some resort near Disney-World, a time share deal that was arranged by my friend and real estate agent Tom for buying my home in Roscoe, Pa. in 2008.

I made arrangements with George to visit him at his home in Daytona Beach after our time at the resort.

Marcia and I arrived at the resort late in the evening that first day, and it was a hassle from the very beginning!

Confusion over which hotel room we were assigned to would take over an hour before we finally got our room.

In the morning I was so hungry but we were told that we couldn't have breakfast until we attended a seminar and watch a movie on how to buy one of these time shares.

Then after having only a continental style breakfast of doughnuts and fruit,

No eggs to order, no pancakes!

We then were led by some woman to see all of the fascinating aspects of owning these time shares, this woman was nice enough but persisted that we buy one.

Believe it or not, the price of one of these deals went from $35,000 to a much lower price of $15,000 by the end of the three hour ordeal,

So much for the time share fascination back then!

Of course we still didn't buy.

There was no lunch or dinner included so we ate at a Denny's, later we went to Publix's, a grocery store chain in Florida to buy a can of coffee, some powdered Creamer and coffee filters, we also bought tea bags and a small box of sugar cubes for Marcia.

Our hotel room had a coffee maker but had nothing for it,

I just can't function without my morning coffee!

At least the hotel had a swimming pool and I enjoyed that late in the evening!

Marcia and I drove to Lake Land, Florida the next morning after having our coffee and tea!

I wanted to see if I could find another old friend of mine from the past at a flea market there, I couldn't find 'Hal', I learned that he quit the flea market business and was at that time selling Gold on the internet. The trip wasn't a complete waste of time though; Marcia bought a bunch of VHS Disney movies to sell at the flea market, including the very collectable one,

'Little Mermaid!'

If you don't know why it's collectable, it's because the cover artist was in some kind of contractual disagreement with Disney, or so I was told!

The artist actually designed the artwork with a slightly hidden Penis!

Nearly a million of these were sold before Disney found out, so they were all pulled from the stores and destroyed, then Disney revised and reprinted the cover and put out 'Little Mermaid II'

Marcia and I drove back to our hotel after having dinner late in the evening and stayed our second night.

After waking up the next morning and again having our coffee and tea, Marcia and I bagged up our belongings and cleaned up our room.

When we went straight to the hotel desk in the morning to 'check out,'

No breakfast what so ever this time!

We learned that we couldn't leave until our room was checked!

"Did they think I would carry out the television or the refrigerator from the hotel?"

I Escaped the Grip of the Grim Reaper

Marcia and I sat in the lobby for nearly thirty minutes until we were free to leave. What a hassle the whole experience turned out to be!

We finally left the hotel and drove to George's.

When we arrived, Raymond, George's brother and also my old friend that I haven't seen for all of those years either also came by.

It was like a family reunion. Ray also lived in Florida at the time in Ormond Beach, just a few miles north. The three of us along with Marcia had a couple of beers; George was drinking shots of Jack Daniels. We all laughed talking about the good old days.

George showed us his rather nice double-wide trailer in this gated community! Yes, a trailer in a gated community, I never heard of such a thing!

George showed me his huge safe loaded with sixty five guns; He is you might say, a gun enthusiast!

He showed me this derringer; he then showed me a twelve gage shot gun.

Soon we all sat at George's dining room table and ate his home made, Pigs in a blanket!

That's what we old 'Hunkys,' call stuffed cabbage!

We later drank beer and shot pool at the community entertainment building, often going outside by the swimming pool to have a cigarette. While we were shooting pool inside, suddenly the trash can outside was on fire.

Marcia emptied an ashtray too soon!

George tossed it into the pool;

It was so funny!

George jumped into the pool to grab the trash can and handed it to Ray as he gathered up all of the burned papers and such. Marcia was so shaken up!

She almost cried!

I would tease her about it for a long time!

Later that night Ray left, leaving me and Marcia alone with crazy George. This man of sixty years is still wild and he has lived a wild life. He is suffering with a bad liver from drinking and has hepatitis B, but at his age and health he can still take a man's legs out with one quick move.

He has done well for himself owning his own sewer company named Clog busters; he lives for the moment driving off on vacation on his Harley at any given time.

He also once died and was given last rights from a motor cycle accident some thirty years ago; he has titanium pins in both of his shoulders and both legs.

As the three of us were sitting at his dining room table still drinking and listening to loud AC-DC music, George gets up saying he wanted to show me something. He then goes to his safe and brings over a metal box, he opens it and says,

"Robert, take some!"

The box was loaded with cash and $50 gold coins, he sat down all excited that I was there with him after all of those years, again he yelled,

"Go ahead, I have $50,000 here, you're my friend, take some money," he then grabs a handful of gold coins, throws them on the table and pushes them towards me.

I said,

"Yeah, I take these and you'll shoot me in the morning!" we both laughed, I told him to put his box back into his safe.

We all eventually showered and went to our rooms for the night. Marcia and I left to drive back to North Carolina early the next morning.

Now that I'm writing this book and wanting my models back someday, they sell for $50 on e-bay today. I thought I'd give old George a call to ask if he'd help me to pay for some of them since he tried to push his money on me that time, just to see how sincere he was.

I sure can't buy them! I have a shoe box full of un-opened hospital bills even though I had insurance.

The co-payments must be huge. George denied ever shooting them up with his BB gun. I talked to his brother Ray, living back up here in Monroeville Pa. these days, about George shooting up my models, and he remembers it very well.

Ray and I met for lunch the day I set up at the flea market where Frank works some times. He confirmed that,

"Sure, George shot up your monsters, he just doesn't want to admit it," I called George again and left a message,

I Escaped the Grip of the Grim Reaper

"George you need to fess up, Ray also remembers that it was you and my brother that shot up my models and you were probably the instigator in this dastardly deed, I know we were just kids then but I never took anything of yours out of your house,"

I said other things like,

"You need to cleanse your spirit before you die!"

I wasn't mad or anything, I was actually laughing as I went on and on, he has a short time limit on his messages so I went on until I left four messages. He called me the next morning laughing too! He still insisted that he didn't remember doing such a thing. Well that's enough of that, perhaps he'll remember someday, it was a long time ago!

I want these models back and a shelf for them, I guess I just started my new 'Bucket list.'

I recently had an episode that brought me down to reality. The State Police were called to one of my two unit rentals, and were called again the very next day; I was in the process of evicting the lady tenant living in the smaller apartment for non- payment of rent and most importantly for disturbing the peace.

This woman in the smaller apartment was continually drinking and yelling to herself, 'nobody else lived there,' and pounding on the walls, just to harass my other tenant all day and night.

Then this woman came outside as Robin, my other tenant and her four-teen year old son Cody, were just coming home from a long days' work and picking her Cody up from his dads' house. She screamed,

"I'm going to kill you, you fat bitch!"

This happened two days in a row, this woman was warned by the police the first day, and finally she was arrested the next day.

How am I supposed to now have this new and beautiful life when it's shrouded by something like this! I will journey on!

The old me would have worried the entire time of the eviction process that she was putting holes in my walls, or bleaching my carpets deliberately, now I feel that I'll cross that bridge when it's necessary, why worry over something I have no control over!

As it turns out, there is yet another silver lining to this story as well. This woman moved out of the apartment voluntarily one day, she left the keys on the outside wall. There were no holes in the walls, and she didn't bleach my carpets but lots of trash to bag up, and she abandoned her cat.

I heard whimpering in the same area that I found my Buffy some four years ago. I unlocked the shed and there she was; this cute cat, grey and brown in color. She was hiding behind my rider mower. I took her home and put out some cat food and water for her. After two days of just leaving her alone while she stayed under my bed she suddenly jumped onto my bed with me purring tremendously!

We soon bonded and I then saw that she was pregnant, she gave birth to four kittens three days later, the day after Mothers' Day.

How's that for fate? Now, not only did I have a new friend, I had five new friends! I would eventually give away three of the kittens.

I call both of my new cats Buffy, I don't think they mind! That way, they both come to me when I call them, LOL!

After three weeks of first seeing my friend Frank again from the flea market he called, I asked him why he never called me to have his oil pan gasket replaced, he replied,

"Bob, I just didn't want you to pay for it," I said,

"I know Frank, but did you ever have it fixed?"

He answered,

"No, but now the fluid is pouring out of the power steering pump," and he needed $150 to have it fixed. He said he would pay me back the following week when he got his SSI check, I told him,

"Of course I'll loan you the money, but can you drive the van to the flea market this Saturday?"

He replied,

"Sure I can."

I told him that I was going to the flea market rain or shine to set up. I told him that we could set up together and I'd look at the pump and replace it after the day of selling at one of my rentals not far from the flea market.

At least that was the plan for that Saturday, I drove forty miles in my big gas sucking van to this flea market in the cold, only to see that Frank wasn't there waiting, I took a rental space and called him. He was still sleeping, what nerve I thought!

I Escaped the Grip of the Grim Reaper

I'm here at seven o'clock in the freezing morning not so much for myself to make money but to help my friend. I parked my van and called his house, his wife answered,

"Is Frank there?" I asked,

"He's sleeping!" she answered.

I told her I was waiting for him at the flea market, and asked if she would let him know.

I set up and started to sell. An hour or so later Frank came walking towards me, I asked him where his mini-van was, he said he didn't have anything to sell so he just parked it in the customer parking lot, I told him that was fine,

"We'll look at it later." I said.

He complained that it was too cold and that he'd rather have a mechanic fix it near his home adding that he had a bad feeling that we would tear down the engine and not be able to put it back together, and he'd be stuck out there thirty miles from his home.

I sort of agreed with him. So much for making plans! The high temperature was forecast to be in the high forty's but I don't think it reached thirty-five degrees. It's almost the month of May!

"That's Pittsburgh weather for you!"

As the both of us sat in my running van for heat occasionally going out to help a customer, I asked Frank if it was true that the bronze statue that he found and sold for $2,700 some years ago was indeed from the Sung Dynasty, and if it was he had made a big mistake!

I told him that I looked it up on the internet. I told him that this Sung Dynasty was from the twelfth century. I asked if there was a head broken off or something, he said it was in perfect condition, just needed to be dusted off!

I kidded with him all that morning saying that what he had was probably priceless! He said that I was,

"Rubbing it in!"

I soon after making only $150 for the day made the decision to quit for the day, business was slow due to the cold and Frank helped me to pack up. I went to hand him the $150, but he only wanted $100 saying that he had the rest; he added that he would pay me back.

I told him it may be a while before I drive forty miles, pay the rental, and make only $150 or so, jokingly adding,

"And give it to you!" He said he'd mail the money to me,

I said, "Don't worry about it." He hugged me saying,

"Bob, you saved me again, thanks a lot!"

After the flea market I stopped by Bobby's, my step son. Yes, I still call him my stepson even though I wasn't ever married to Marcia and I don't even see her anymore.

It was just after twelve noon, Bobby, his wife Janet and I were talking, his two daughters were up playing with their little salt and pepper 'mostly pepper' kittens.

Savanna or 'Anna' the youngest daughter was laying on the couch snuggled in a blanket with one of the kittens suffering with Laryngitis.

We talked for a while about a lot of things, then Bobby asked if I knew that Ashley, Marcia's grand-daughter was pregnant. I told him,

"No, I didn't know!" I then added, "That's nice, she's not even married!"

Bobby then said,

"Oh, she got married while she was in Hawaii back in October, before you and Mom went to North Carolina for the winter!"

Bobby then made some hamburgers for lunch; I soon left to drive the thirty-five more miles to my home in Roscoe.

On the way home I was thinking about how Marcia didn't mention any of this to me, realizing again how secretive she was. Perhaps she had plans to be more involved with Ashley and her new baby, since I was also told that Ashley's husband is a military man stationed in Hawaii for quite some time.

When I first met Marcia in 2001, she was often babysitting her then eight grand-children; I guess I took her away from much of this in our new relationship. I soon realized that this might have been the reason why we weren't getting along also. Maybe this is why Marcia was put on this earth; after all she is the mother hen type.

And at the age of sixty-four, she doesn't want me interfering. I just hope for the best for her!

One Friday morning I went to the Post Office to check my P.O. for my mail, in this little town of Roscoe, there is no mail delivery, everybody has a PO Box.

I Escaped the Grip of the Grim Reaper

When I first bought this house in 2008, I went to the local Walmart, bought a mail box and asked this neighbor,

"Hi, can you tell me which side of the house I should put up this mail box?"

The nice elderly woman just laughed,

"Oh my, we don't have mail delivery! You have to get your own PO Box!"

Again, I never heard of such a thing! I returned the box to Walmart, and went to the Post office and got my P.O. Box!

Anyway, as I was walking out the door of the Post Office I see Nancy, my brief tenant of two months; she was parked right behind my van standing by her opened side door where she had her youngest daughter strapped in a car seat. I yelled out,

"Hey Nancy!" she of course said, "Hi Bob!"

Suddenly she screamed out,

"Bob, I think I just got stung!" I hurried over to her,

"Bob, it's in my pants!"

I pulled her shorts down and flicked the Yellow Jacket bee from her behind, the swelling already had started, Nancy then fell to the floor of the mini-van crying,

"Where's my EPI- pen?" I found this gizmo under her passenger seat.

"Is this it?" I cried out! Nancy became in-coherent, babbling,

"I don't know how to use it, I could die!" I called 911 from my cell phone, and had someone on the phone telling me how to use the thing!

I then took the blue cap off and thrust it on Nancy's thigh! I then told him where we were.

He said an ambulance was on the way. I stayed on the phone with this man, with him asking how she was; she then fell onto the side walk mumbling with her face covered with sweat, the man said that her heart was probably racing and told me to try to keep her calm! Nancy's baby then began to cry.

It was truly a hectic situation!

The ambulance soon arrived. Two paramedics came to us. Nancy, not wanting to go to the hospital argued,

"I'm ok, I'm ok!" As she was being strapped into a stretcher I assured Nancy that I would park her car away from the entrance of the Post Office and I would wait for her phone call to come to the hospital when she was released!

The woman paramedic then took Nancy's baby and car seat and strapped it to the floor of the ambulance.

After the ambulance left I parked Nancy's van across the street and took her key into the post office for them to have in case it had to be moved. I explained what had happened and then went home to await Nancy's call.

Nancy called an hour or so later, and I drove the eight miles to pick her up. On the way back to the Post Office to get her key Nancy kept saying things like,

"You're my hero!" and

"It is fate that I met you, you just saved my life!"

I got a little teary eyed thinking that maybe it really was an act of God that I came back from the dead, perhaps to save this young woman's life some day.

It's also fate that Nancy moved out of my home in Roscoe also. I decided to put the home on the market for I no longer want to be a land-lord, just more of my need to have a new and beautiful life.

I called Tom my real estate friend to list it, I met him at the home and he took eighteen pictures. I thought eighteen photos, isn't that too much?

Or are that many photos over doing it? In the game of real estate the home is listed at a certain price then you go from there, you hardly ever get that price! You listen to offers then the seller counter-offers.

Three or four days after the home was listed Tom calls me, I was at the out-door pool at the YMCA, he tells me that there was a contract signed for my home, from a different agent from a different real estate firm and the buyer agreed to the listed price.

Tom went on to tell that the prospective buyer was living in York, Pa. and this buyers fiancée was soon starting college at CALU, a local small university in California Pa. in September and he agreed to buy my home solely on the eighteen photos. I was in complete disbelief! Things just don t work out that way for me, I kept saying to Tom,

"Quit pulling my leg!"

Then Tom would say,

"No Bob, I'm serious, the house is sold!"

I Escaped the Grip of the Grim Reaper

I was so happy! Tom then added that the new owner only wanted me to provide a refrigerator and a stove, not new but nice used appliances, I agreed of course. I also did quite a few other things since I got my asking price.

I had Bobby, Marcia's son put in a glass block window in the basement, a newer window in the bathroom of the little apartment that I lived in, and lots of other things and a new toilet seat.

I wound up moving into the apartment of the evicted tenant that I previously wrote about. Things are finally starting to go my way, Marcia my ex-fiancée, helped a lot in cleaning up my Roscoe home and cleaning out the garage and the shed. A lot of the things belonged to her anyway!

I've been going to the YMCA to swim at the out-door pool a lot this summer, it's been really hot and humid but it's really boring, kids, kids and more kids, not that I don't like kids but they come in droves and I'm trying to meet a lady.

It was about the third time there when I met Denny, a tall athletic looking sixty-five year old fellow. I was wading in the four foot section of the pool when I heard someone yell out,

"Is the water real cold?" I look over to this man saying,

"No, it's not cold at all!" he then yelled out,

"I can dig it!"

I then cried out,

"Man, I haven't heard that expression for a long, long time!"

This guy then jumps into the water and that was the start of our friendship!

He is an odd man, always telling me of his proud heritage of being 'Russian.' For sixty-five he's a good looking man, and he still has all of his curly hair. He thenstarts to sing something about his Jewish girl friend, and words of the 70's rock band, 'Black Sabbath.'

Then I started to also sing their song 'War Pigs,' Generals gather in their masses, just like witches at black masses, he again yells,

"I can dig it!" We talk, he says he used to be a singer for a rock and roll band years ago, and nowadays he sings at Karaoke bars, and that really got my interest for I no longer sing with Sonny at his Karaoke gigs.

He told me of a bar in Monongahela Pa. called Eck's and says there was Karaoke that coming Thursday night. I went home and looked up the bar on the internet for directions and soon there I was singing again!

The disc jockey is a man and wife team and they call themselves, White Rose!

Denny is a real good singer, loud and he's a performer like me; we argue who is better!

I think he is! He is wild though, he takes his shoes off and sings barefooted, and get this! He likes to pull his pants down, not all of the way but enough to make the patrons laugh and clap, he's always being told to behave himself!

Paula, the wife of White Rose told me that Denny's mom died not too long ago and he's taking it pretty bad, and that is partly why he gets a little crazy!

After that first Thursday night, I didn't see Denny at the pool all week! When I saw him again at Karaoke he told me he got thrown out of the YMCA, for what? You guessed it 'for pulling down his bathing shorts,' he cried out,

"I was wearing a thong underneath my swimming shorts!"

I said, "Denny, that's still in-appropriate with all of the children there! He argued,

"I had the longest running membership since 1976!" and added,

"That's thirty-six years Bob!"

I told him he should apologize and try to get re-instated for which he agreed but he got thrown out again a week later for the same thing.

So, I still go to the pool without old Denny being there and like I said it's boring with mostly kids, until I met Suzy,

I went one day and a nice looking lady was there with her grand-son, she was laying on the grass on her stomach as her grand-son was in the water. We eventually made eye-contact and she smiled, I climbed out of the pool and sat at the bench next to her,

"Hi, how are you?" she smiled, I then asked,

"Is that your son that you're with?" she laughed,

"No, he's my grand-son!"

I then said,

"You don't look old enough to have a grand-son!" she just ate that right up saying,

"Thank you very much!"

I Escaped the Grip of the Grim Reaper

I introduced myself and told her I was a new member and of course I told her of me dying, the whole coma thing and that I was writing a book about it! Suzy seemed interested.

I asked her if she ever was at Eck's for Karaoke, she replied,

"Yes, but it's been a while!"

I told her that I sing, I even sung a few lyrics, "Seven lonely days and a dozen towns ago, I reached out one night and you were gone!" Suzy asked,

"Isn't that Elvis Presley?" I answered,

"Yes, Kentucky Rain!" She then said that I sounded pretty good, I said,

"You should come out tomorrow night!" she then said,

"Maybe I will call a few of my girlfriends and do just that!"

Just then a horde of children came running into the place they were all around me. I decided to leave telling Suzy that I had steaks and ribs out in the hot car and that I'd better get them home! I told her that is was nice talking to her, adding that I hoped I would see her soon at the bar.

One day I decided that I just had to go to Kennywood, I haven't really found a girlfriend yet, and I haven't come across Suzy yet! I could have gone with my friend Stanley or even with an old friend Lori, but I went alone.

This past summer weather in Pittsburgh has been terrible, we were in a drought as most of the country, I heard that the corn crop is destroyed and the prices for everything associated with corn will be high. I didn't arrive until late in the afternoon, I wanted it to me more of an evening event so it wouldn't be so hot!

I figured that I might meet someone this way too!

So I went! I walked around and I literally would ask certain ladies to ride with me, or sit at one of the many metal benches and ask as they would walk by. I soon saw an attractive lady of fifty years or so walking with a young couple. I said,

"Excuse me, could you ride the Racer with me?" The woman answered,

"Sure, I also need someone to ride with!"

The line was pretty long so I was able to talk to her and we 'clicked,' her name is Carol, after we rode the roller coaster we along with her daughter and her daughters' boy-friend rode the Log Jammer, a kind of roller coaster that splashes in the water after a fifty-three foot drop, we all got pretty wet. After that ride Carol and I went on our own riding the famous roller coaster Thunder-Bolt, and then the Sky Rocket coaster!

The Sky Coaster really terrified me when we dropped into an almost complete vertical drop of ninety-five feet, but after dying and all,

"Who cares?"

We then rode the Train, one of the oldest rides at Kennywood, it's a slow harmless train, and you can see my hometown of Braddock from across the river on the ride.

When we finally found the new ride 'Black Widow,' it was shut down for the day because of mechanical problems, the working crew had it running for a while with no one on the ride, but they never opened it, it's really a good thing because after seeing it swing back and forth and spin high into the sky I don't think I would have rode it anyway!

A lot of people that I talked to were very upset about it not being open too!

Two of the things I like most to do when I go to Kennywood is to have some Pizza and the other is to have a Dip Cone with nuts and a cherry stuck on top with a tooth pick at the end of the long day!

I was amazed when Carol said the same thing, we first had a large slice of Pizza, and later in the evening after going on about ten other rides often taking a break to sit and talk because of my still sore and tired legs we had our ice cream.

Carol and I soon met up with her daughter at the exit of the park, Carol gave me her phone number, we softly kissed and I walked away, leaving the park! I will soon call and ask if she would like to go jet skiing! I hope it all goes well with Carol!

This is an amazing story for both men 'and not to be a male chauvinist' women who are carpenters!

This past Labor Day weekend for which marks the second anniversary of the fire at my flea market, my ex-step son 'so to speak' and my friend Bobby along with his two girls were invited to go to his boss's house for a swim. This awesome huge in-ground pool was built using only outdoor treated boards and treated plywood as the walls and floor inside of the pool by Bobby's boss Bill Lasko, some thirty years ago, and it's still in perfect condition, and the vinyl pool liner is still as tight as can be.

Bill also built a ten foot high diving platform, I chose to jump from it instead of diving because I now have a bad shoulder, I can't raise my right

I Escaped the Grip of the Grim Reaper

arm without feeling excruciating pain which may require surgery, hopefully I just need a few cortisone shots and physical therapy!

But I was daring to even jump from the ten foot platform.

Between Bill's pool, a public pool not far from where I live and the YMCA I must have went swimming fifty times this past summer, now that's having fun!

A far cry from not going at all for the two previous years!

Nowadays I watch the Comedy Central television station a lot and I love the Tosh.O show!

This one episode that I just watched shows a woman sticking a pencil into some mans huge 'Boil' on his back, it was so gross that I almost 'threw up,' when this green puss spewed from the wound, the woman then squeezed this massive infection again and more of this green puss came squirting out!

It was so awful but funny at the same time!

My mother once told me of a time when I was just a child, I also had a boil removed but from my 'ass,' at the Braddock Hospital and it took four nurses to hold me down!

I just had to mention this Tosh.O show, perhaps you have seen it, if not you just have to watch it one night!

In one last story-line of my loving daughter! The case is still on-going; I have attorney Mr. Peter Daley, he's also a Pennsylvania State Legislator.

Although she did save my life, for which of course, I am very grateful for, she had no right to steal my money!

I would have given her the money and more for her expenses to drive to North Carolina!

Well my book is just about complete, I will go to the Grand Canyon soon, perhaps with Carol or maybe with Suzy or somebody else, who knows?

I will also soon be riding a jet ski somewhere too!

In closing I'd like to say that I'm so happy to be alive, I'm singing Karaoke again, and if there is one song that best describes my life, it's Bob Seger's signature song,

"Turn the Page!"

I just wish I can sing it to you!

"Here I am, I'm on the road again, here I am, I'm up on the stage, and there I go, playing that star again, there I go, turn the page!"

No matter what life demands, we should all take a deep breath while we're stuck in traffic or where ever we are, look around, look into the sky, and say to ourselves!

"I'm here and life is beautiful!"

I think we should all die once and be lucky enough to come back to life and have a second chance.

If only we could all do this, maybe we would have a better attitude and be nicer to each other, the world would be a much better place to live!

Goodbye and thanks for reading my book!

The End!

Please e-mail me at ralee5@yahoo.com if you wish. Thanks again!!!!!!

CPSIA information can be obtained
at www.ICGtesting.com
Printed in the USA
LVHW050110240322
714169LV00008B/377

9 781475 261264